On the
SUNNYSIDE
of Life

*A collection of short stories about life on
an isolated cattle ranch in eastern Nevada*

SALLY WHIPPLE MOSHER MOONEY

To order additional copies of this book, contact:
Xlibris Corporation
1-888-795-4274
www.Xlibris.com
Orders@Xlibris.com
113218

Acknowledgments

I thank my friends and family who have listened to me tell them for twelve years that I am "writing my book." They all finally got so tired of hearing about it that they took action to get it published. Thanks to my sister, Bonnie, who bought me a new computer, and to friends Carol, and Pat, who did editing and encouraging. Thanks to Bob and Kathryn who made the publishing possible. Thanks to Lesley, my daughter, who spent many hours organizing my stories and pictures for publishing; and to Julie, my niece, who was 'on call' to scan pictures and help with computer problems. It took a village!

I'm dedicating my book to Betty Isaacs (Liz Risedan) who was a wonderful writer and who read every story and remembers being on the ranch much of the time. She did not live to see this book, but I would not have written it without her wisdom and encouragement.

KEEP ON THE SUNNYSIDE

Written by: A.P. Carter/ Peer Music International Corp (BMI)
Sung by June Carter Cash

Well there's a dark and troubled side of life
There's a bright and sunny side too
But if you meet with the darkness and strife
The sunny side we also may view

Keep on the sunny side, always on the sunny side
Keep on the sunny side of life
It will help us every day, it will brighten all the way
If we'll keep on the sunny side of life

Though the storm and its fury broke today
Crushing hopes that I cherish so dear
Clouds and storms will in time pass away
The sun again will shine bright and clear

Keep on the sunny side, always on the sunny side
Keep on the sunny side of life
It will help us every day, it will brighten all the way
If we'll keep on the sunny side of life

Let us greet with a song of hope each day
Though the moments be cloudy or fair
Let us trust in our Savior always
To keep us every one in His care

Keep on the sunny side, always on the sunny side
Keep on the sunny side of life
It will help us every day, it will brighten all the way
If we'll keep on the sunny side of life

Prologue

"We have to open a window; we're going to pass out back here; it's so hot," we would yell from the back seat of our 1942 Mercury as my brother and I bumped along listening to the deafening sound of gravel crashing against the bottom of the car. Then Mom would turn the window handle ever so slightly. Immediately, dust began pouring up through the floorboard making it almost impossible to breathe or see.

"Close the windows," Daddy would holler from the front seat, "We're choking to death." This went on for the entire thirty-five miles of dirt road from the small farming community of Lund, Nevada, to our ranch at Sunnyside. If we saw a car leaving Lund ahead of us, we'd need to wait five or ten minutes to give it a head start so we wouldn't "eat their dust." Thick clouds of dust billowing up behind a car for miles made it impossible to pass. Eventually I'd catch site of the line of cottonwood trees growing along the creek at our ranch. I always thought it was the most beautiful sight on earth. It was an oasis in a huge alkali desert.

I hated those stifling hot, dusty trips to town. It got so I flat refused to go to Lund and then on to Ely whenever my parents needed to get staples and do banking. My dad would try to bribe me into going to town. "We can stop at the Ely Drug Store and get a marshmallow nut sundae," he'd say. It didn't work. Truthfully, I hated leaving the ranch. I knew from my first memory that I wanted to live at Sunnyside for the rest of my life. ! I loved the wide-open spaces and the freedom to roam the vast distances in every direction; the outdoor life with definite seasons, and the beautiful white sage flat. I loved the cattle drives and all of our animals - horses, cows, sheep, dogs, cats, chickens and ducks. Even wild animals like rabbits, deer, coyotes, bobcats, mountain lions and snakes were part of our lives. I loved swimming at Hot Creek and exploring the Whipple Cave my grandfather and Uncle Vern discovered. Watching the atomic bombs go off just 100 miles from the Nevada Test Site in the 1950's was exciting. I loved working side by side with my family to make our ranch one of the most beautiful places in the White River Valley.

Sunnyside is in Nye County, Nevada. It is on the old maps of Nevada because the original settlement served as a post office in the 1890's. It became Sunnyside Whipple Ranch in 1904 when Grandpa bought it. It stayed in the family after my father took it over and extended the range rights to run as many as 3000 head of cattle. Isolation was very much a part of life at Sunnyside. In my father's time, there were ten children in his family to play together, go to school with, and to keep each other company. However, the first ten years of my brother Warner's and my lives, we had no one but each other and the animals to keep us company. There was no community, no church and few neighbors. Warner and I were usually the only two students at the school on the ranch. Seldom did a car drive by on the dusty, rutted road.

My father sold Sunnyside in 1962 because my brother was not interested in staying there. Even though I asked to take the ranch, I did not get that chance. Females didn't own or run ranches according to my father.... Especially not his daughter who was to be a lady - not "a broken down old cowboy."

Now, when I read stories of women on ranches, I wonder if I should consider myself a ranch woman at all. I lost that life when I was twenty years old. Then I realize in my heart I have never left the ranch. It is where I will always be. If you've ever lived a cowboy life, it will forever define who you are. Those years defined who I am from my work ethic to my love of being outdoors and alone. The spirit of the west is alive and well in me. I've worked to turn every place I've ever lived into Sunnyside. By reading the stories I've written, I'm hoping my readers will feel some connection to a life I thought was so special.

Part One
An Isolated Life

1   *The Road to Sunnyside*

JL Whipple, my grandfather, rode alone on horseback with no extra clothes or food—only a canteen of water—from St. George, Utah, to Lund, Nevada. It was the spring of 1898, and the LDS Church had recently settled three towns: Lund, Preston, and Georgetown (later Ely) in the White River Valley, Nevada, and had hired Grandpa to take charge of the ranch and cattle in that valley. When he got to Pioche, he realized he had no idea how to get to Lund or Preston or even the White River Valley. A stage driver told him to keep riding west, which he did. One night, he rode toward a tiny light up ahead and found it was a trapper's campfire. He camped there that night and then continued riding. Along the way, he made a mental note of promising outcroppings where he planned to come back and check out for gold or silver. JL did many things in his lifetime, but prospecting remained his greatest passion.

Sunnyside was the first inhabited settlement he came upon during his long ride. He remembered it as a pretty place with water coming from three freshwater springs and a nice-sized creek flowing right by the back door of the cabin. The water was the clearest and coldest he'd ever seen.

On April 17, 1898, five days after leaving Pioche, he made it to Lund. There he met another colonizer who'd arrived the same night from Salt Lake City. Together they worked for a month, gathering 1200 head of cattle and driving them to the Ephraim Mountains near Salt Lake City. After bringing the saddle horses back to Lund, Grandpa rigged up an outfit and left for St. George to move his family to Nevada.

He moved his mother, Caroline; his younger sister, Effie; Grandma Rose Ellen; their two sons, Murray and Laverne; and their three-month-old daughter, Eliza Dent. All these people and their "earthly possessions" were in one wagon, and it took six days to get to Lund. They carried water for drinking and for the horses in a barrel wired to the side of the wagon. The

1

water ran out after two nights, and the situation was grave when they made it to the Silver King Well. It was full of dead rats and mice, but there was no other water, so Grandpa let himself down into the well. He and Effie bailed the water out with a bucket. Then Grandpa was able to make a new hole in the side of the well and get freshwater for camp use. Grandma never forgot the horrifying night they all spent in a shack used to store horse hides. Coyotes were used to feasting on the hides, so hundreds of them swarmed the shack, clawing at the door and howling all night long. The adults kept a fire going and took turns trying to sleep and beating on cans and buckets to keep them away.

They moved into an old one-room log cabin when they got to Lund. Six people and a tiny baby had to make-do for the winter while Grandpa got busy with the cattle he'd been hired to run for the Mormon Church.

In the spring, Grandpa and three men took wagons to Taylor, twenty miles away, where he'd bought a lumber house. They tore it all apart and hauled it back to Lund, rebuilt it, and it became JL's family home—the first lumber house in Lund. It was also my grandmother's first home.

Grandmother Rose Ellen had been raised in foster homes in St. George before she was married. She and her brother, William, were brought to America by Mormon missionaries when they were ages five and seven. It was not unusual for poor coal-mining families from Wales to "send their children out" by ships to a relative in America after the family was converted to the Mormon Church. These children were being taken across the ocean in hopes that a better life would greet them in America. Their families would follow them to America some time later.

When the children got to St. George where their grandmother lived, there was a problem. She had thought the children were older, so they could help her. She would not take the children. Grandma lived with whatever family would take her in until she was old enough to work for her board and room. Her life was tough as she moved from one family to another. She dropped out of school before the eighth grade because she didn't have decent clothes or shoes. William had the same kind of life. He never married and was buried in the indigent part of the cemetery in Elko, Nevada. Neither he nor Rose Ellen ever saw or heard from their family in Wales again.

Grandma remained devoted to her church for the rest of her life. We believe that is where she met Grandpa. He had a bad heart and was told he would not live long. Grandma loved him and wanted to be with him for whatever time he had left. They were married in the St. George Temple. He died at age ninety-three, outliving Grandma by almost thirty years.

While living in the house in Lund, Grandpa and Grandma had three more daughters: Leone, Beulah, and Vivian (Jo). During that time, Grandpa ran cattle for the church, bought and sold the Barnes Ranch, and hauled in another building from Taylor which he turned into a store, selling dry goods and groceries.

One day, Grandpa ran across the stage driver who carried mail and supplies south from Lund to Sharp (now Adaven) by way of Sunnyside. The driver told Grandpa that Mr. Horton, who owned Sunnyside, had recently lost his wife and no longer had any interest in staying on the place. He wanted to sell out.

The next morning, Grandpa saddled his horse and rode the thirty-five miles south from Lund to Sunnyside. He had not forgotten the place he'd seen when he first rode into Nevada several years before. Mr. Horton was so anxious to sell Sunnyside; he thought of a way for Grandpa to buy the ranch without much money. Mr. Horton suggested that Grandpa could feed the thirty head of steers that went with the ranch through the winter, sell them in the spring, and give him the money as a down payment for the ranch. Using Mr. Horton's own steers for the down payment on the ranch was a deal too good to pass up. The deal was sealed with a handshake. Sunnyside had now become the Sunnyside Whipple Ranch which is on present-day maps.

The day after Christmas 1904, JL and Grandmother Rose Ellen loaded up their belongings and left Lund with the first six of their ten children to begin their life at Sunnyside. It was bitter cold. The first day they made it to a little ranch called Six Mile where they camped that night. Four little girls, one an infant, crouched under quilts in the bottom of the buckboard. Every few miles, they would stop and build a fire to heat rocks which they put on the floor of the wagon to keep Eliza Dent, six; Leone, four; Beulah, two; and baby Vivian, two months, from freezing. The boys, Murray and Laverne, ages ten and eight, drove the one hundred head of cattle. They were all nearly frozen when they got to the Riordan Ranch. Jim Riordan saw them coming. "My god," he said in his especially loud, high voice. "Get on down and come inside before you all freeze to death." The cattle were corralled for the night, and the young boys came inside with the rest of the family. Their hands and feet were frostbitten. The Riordan home was like heaven to my grandparents and their children after being out in the biting cold for two days and a night.

The next morning, they made the last twelve miles to Sunnyside. The wagon rocked and bounced as they slowly moved south on the deeply rutted, narrow road. After they passed the cedars (a clump of trees just beyond Riordan Ranch), the white sage flat loomed ahead of them for as far as they could see. They caught sight of the cottonwood trees at Sunnyside five miles before they got there. It was after dark when they got to the tiny cabin which was to be their new home.

Grandma had not been happy to make the trip in the winter, but she immediately changed when she saw Sunnyside with the three freshwater springs that did not vary in winter or summer, the watercress-filled creek flowing right next to the cabin, the cottonwood trees, the majestic purple mountains east of the cabin, and the beautiful White River Valley expanding almost forever to the west. She fell in love with the place and was happy to live there for the rest of her life.

Sunnyside 1904

J.L. and Rose Ellen wedding picture

2 Sunnyside Whipple Ranch

The family made it through that first winter in the two-room log cabin using one room for cooking and eating and one for sleeping. Grandma had a shelf for a cupboard, a wood-burning cookstove which kept the small room warm, and a table and chairs in her kitchen. There was an outhouse below the creek.

In the spring, before Grandpa added any rooms to the house, he built a long, spacious stone barn with a tin roof. That was in keeping with his philosophy "A barn is more valuable than a house on a ranch. It protects the animals, and the animals are a necessity." Even when the ranch house was finished, it had less square footage than the barn.

Also that spring, he and his boys planted a long row of Lombardy poplars (Mormon trees) along the bank of the creek that flowed north through the meadow. There are only theories about why Mormon people always planted these trees along ditch banks and streets like stately figures "marching with God" wherever they settled. Poplars are fast-growing slender, tall trees that require little care. "They look heavenward, but their roots are in the earth." Mormon people look toward heaven while believing they can also create a bit of heaven for themselves from the earth.

Grandpa fed Mr. Horton's cattle until April of that first year. Then he and Murray drove them to Delamor, a mining camp, sold them, and got the money to Mr. Horton. He managed to keep making the payments on the ranch one way or another. He got a mail contract between Pioche and Sunnyside. It was over fifty miles, a two-day trip by buggy, so he kept a fresh horse halfway. On one trip, the spare horse had gotten away. He noticed an interesting outcropping of rocks while hunting for that horse. When he had a few samples assayed, he learned it was high-grade silver ore. He located the Silver Horn Mine and later sold it for $10,000—more than enough to pay off the ranch.

Grandpa eventually built a nice-sized dining room one step up from the log kitchen, then a bedroom off each side of that room. The girls slept in one of those bedrooms, and my grandparents had the other bedroom. The boys slept in the original log room off the kitchen which was forever known as "the cold room." It was never insulated nor heated, so it was also used as a cooler for food storage. Daddy told of soogans they'd put over themselves to keep warm. He claimed they were made of canvas filled with rocks. (That was one of many strange stories Daddy used to tell.) The last room Grandpa built was the parlor. It was the nicest room in the house with a bay window facing the front yard and the eastern mountains. Most importantly, it had a separate outside entrance, so my grandfather could entertain his "important guests" without them having to mingle with the common folk (namely his family). Four more children were born at Sunnyside: LaRue, Clair (Punk, my father), Caroline, and Phyllis.

Grandpa built a powerhouse where he placed a generator to be powered by water from the creek. Sunnyside was the first ranch that anybody knew about to have electricity. By moving a headgate, water was rerouted from the large creek into a small ditch to run the generator. Most of the time, the water was not used to light the single bulb hanging from the ceiling in the kitchen because it ran down the main stream to water the meadow land and alfalfa fields below the ranch. He also built several outbuildings on the place, including a rock milk cellar, a granary, a machine shed, a storeroom with a basement underneath to store food, a shop, a saddle house, and a small bunkhouse.

The dining room at Sunnyside was a favorite place for the young people from the other ranches to come to dance and eat. The Whipples were a fun, talented bunch, and the girls were very pretty and good cooks. Grandpa bought Grandma a player piano for the parlor. Murray played several instruments; LaVerne played the violin and harmonica; Punk played the harmonica and sang. Grandma had a beautiful singing voice. They also took turns meeting at the three other ranches in the valley. They'd stop work early on Saturdays, put the washtub of water over a large fire in the yard, and all take baths. Wherever they met, there would be a buffet or sandwiches and desserts at midnight. Many times, they'd keep dancing until morning before climbing into their buckboards and heading home. The Whipple family didn't go to church on Sundays because the trip to Lund was much too far, but they did follow the Mormon custom of relaxing on Sundays—only doing the necessary chores and never starting a new job.

In his early years on the ranch, Grandpa kept up the buildings and spent his time ranching and tending cattle. He also bought another ranch in the valley and then sold it. He still had a 100-acre farm in Lund where he raised five hundred bushels of wheat. He, Ervin Hendrix, and Jim Riordan built a flour mill in Lund. He was appointed postmaster in Sunnyside in 1917. He oversaw four mail routes coming in: one from Sharp, one from Pioche, one from Ely and Lund, and one from Cave Valley. He sold his Lund farm but then bought 1480 acres of meadow land forming the Lund Field. He split this land up and sold it to "the Lund boys" in 1930. He built his cattle up to one thousand head.

During those years, he continued to prospect and finally bought the Silver Horn Mine back. His passion had always been prospecting. He began thinking about retiring from ranching in the 1930s. He wanted to spend his remaining years searching in the hills for another rich find. Sunnyside was showing serious signs of neglect. The ranch was run down and needed plenty of work. Most of the ten children had married and moved away. Grandma was quite heavy and had bad feet. She spent much of her time sitting in the parlor with her needlework, gazing at the mountains.

Grandpa had planned for his oldest son, Murray, who was his favorite, to take over the ranch. Murray and Aunt Ouida had been living in the small bunkhouse on the ranch for ten years. Murray, however, had no desire to take over a ranch as neglected as Sunnyside. He chose to buy the Hiko Ranch seventy-five miles south near the small town of Alamo. By then LaVerne, the next son in line, had returned from World War I. He had been mustard gassed and was missing for almost three years. Part of that time, he was hospitalized. He then wandered throughout Germany looking for his company. Before he found them, the war was over. He stayed on even working as a trick rider in a circus for a while. When he finally made it back to the United States, he married his high school sweetheart, and they bought a farm in Lund. Vern's lungs and limbs had been weakened from the mustard gas, so he was never well after that.

Begrudgingly, Grandpa offered the ranch to my father who was much younger than his two brothers and most of his sisters. According to Grandpa's Puritan-Mormon values, the daughters would not be offered the ranch unless there were no other boys in the family. In 1935, my parents, Clair (Punk) and Lila Robison Whipple, leased and later bought the Sunnyside Whipple Ranch from my grandparents.

Grandpa branding in wool suit

Back of house next to creek 1920's

Mail truck stopping at Sunnyside 1920

3 Sunnyside Whipple Ranch—The Next Generation

"You'll lose your shirt, Lile," Uncle Murray said to my mother one morning as he sat on the edge of the kitchen sink. "I wouldn't touch this run-down old place with a ten-foot pole." My mother informed him that losing their shirt would not be a problem because she and my dad did not even have a shirt that she was aware of. At that time, Daddy was herding sheep for Grandpa.

Everyone in my father's family thought leasing the ranch to him was a bad idea. My dad loved the things money could buy, had chosen not to finish high school because he was homesick, and had borrowed money from Grandpa when he didn't make enough money to pay the debts he had incurred. This was not going to be a success story according to all those who knew my father. But they did not reckon with my mother.

The smartest decision my father ever made was to marry my mother. Without her, he probably would not have become a successful rancher. She was as calm and easygoing as he was volatile. She was practical; he wanted the best of everything. She had a pleasant personality, always doing what she could to help people get along with each other. My dad was fun and charming and a born leader, but he could be a tyrant at times.

My mother kept a promise she'd made to herself when she was very young that she would never fight when she got married. Her parents fought constantly, and she said she'd lived with all the fighting she ever intended to live with. In fact, she remained the mediator in people's lives all of her life. She managed to get along with every one of my dad's seven sisters and was a beloved friend to her sister-in-law. Her mother-in-law confided in her and trusted her completely. Sometimes she would become very discouraged. "It seems like I have spent my whole life trying to make people to get along with each other," she once told me. "Why can't people just be nice to each other?"

Mom and Daddy made the decision together to lease the ranch from Grandpa. Together they dealt with drought, floods, the fluctuating price of cattle, and government land policies. It was not in their plans for my mother to get pregnant with me when Warner was only seven months old, but she got through her pregnancy while cooking for ten or so hired men, tending to the household chores, and caring for a small baby.

My mother once wrote. "Once Clair and I made the decision to lease Sunnyside from the Boss (Clair's father), my life was never the same again. Any work that I had done when I lived with my parents was like a vacation compared to what I did from that point on."

My mother remembered the morning she was bathing Warner in the kitchen sink when Daddy came into the kitchen. "Start packing," he said to Mom. "We're moving." Without consulting their wives, he and Grandpa had decided they were trading houses. Sunnyside now belonged to Mom and Daddy, so it was right they should have the ranch house. At the time, they were living in the small one-bedroom schoolhouse across the creek. Mom quickly dried and powdered Warner, put him in his basket, and began pulling pans and linens out of her cupboards. Grandma had less than a week to move her things out of the big house she'd been living in for thirty years into the small house.

Immediately after they had moved their few possessions into the main house on the ranch, Daddy began to improve it. He added a bathroom with a toilet, a sink, and a clawfoot bathtub. He had better cupboards and a sink installed in the kitchen. He had an eight-foot-long table with benches built for the dining room and put an oil stove in the living room (parlor). It would be several years before they got propane at the ranch, so Mom continued using the wood-burning cookstove. He put a fence around the house, planted grass, iris and yellow rose bushes, and poured a sidewalk to the front gate.

My dad detested junk. He backed his truck up to every building on the place and hauled almost everything up to the dump above the ranch. Many of his sisters were furious that he threw away things they valued, but it was his ranch now, and he could do as he wished. He wished to have a very clean, neat ranch void of the old machinery and other junk found on most ranches. He bought only the best of everything and hauled off anything old or outdated. He was the first rancher in the valley to get a tractor.

Daddy pulled out the Lombardy poplar trees Grandpa had planted along the creek because they used too much water. After he poured a cement ditch and dug a reservoir, he was able to grow acres and acres of alfalfa which we then "hayed" every summer and fed to our cattle all winter. With those trees went any symbolism of Mormonism at Sunnyside. There didn't seem to me to be anything left that represented "marching with God." The cowboy culture, where each day required the same amount of time and work as the day before, took over. Sundays didn't exist anymore. Even Daddy's sisters, who were angry about my dad's "cleaning frenzy," had to admit Sunnyside had gone from a junk pile, when Grandpa owned it and had spent all his time prospecting, to a beautiful place for their families to gather.

My dad always wished his father, the Boss, would make a positive comment to him about the success he'd made of the ranch, but Grandpa never did. Grandma Rose Ellen had a heart attack and died in 1939 at age fifty four. A year later, the Boss married Famie Nelson, a wealthy widow who owned a drugstore in St. George, Utah; and they moved to Ely.

The Boss came to the ranch often while I was growing up. He'd drive up to the front gate, climb out of his big black Cadillac, dust it off with his handkerchief, and walk straight as a rod down the sidewalk to the house. He always wore a three-piece suit with a starched, perfectly ironed white shirt whether he was branding, prospecting, or meeting with important people. He had several old wool suits to work in and one dress suit.

I liked it better when Grandma Famie came to the ranch with him because we'd all play Canasta at the kitchen table in the evenings. Grandmother Rose Ellen died when I was four months old, so Famie was the grandmother I knew, and I liked her very much. I didn't know it then, but I realized later that Grandpa was a nicer person when Grandma Famie was around. My aunts would complain about Famie. "She isn't very nice to Papa," they'd say to my mother.

My mother, who knew better than to have an opinion around any of my dad's seven sisters, would secretly smile. Later she'd say to me, "Yes, the Boss met his match when he married Famie." She remembered how unkind he sometimes was to Rose Ellen. Grandpa knew he'd have to "tow the line" with Famie who he often called "that kid" because she was sixteen years younger than him.

We had many family reunions on the ranch as I was growing up. Grandpa's daughters insisted our family must meet every summer because they'd say, "With Papa's serious heart condition, he won't be living much longer." He lived to be ninety-three, so we ended up having a family reunion every year for over twenty years.

I was surrounded with aunts and uncles who spent weekends and vacations at our ranch. They knew my dad, so they always expected to spend their time working. And they knew my mother, so they knew they'd be eating delicious meals. Everyone came with the idea they'd be helping both my mother and father with the work.

When I get with my cousins nowadays, they usually end up talking about Sunnyside. The older ones worked on the ranch when Grandpa owned it. All of them worked for my dad or mother during the summers at some time in their lives. They say my dad was relentless when it came to work, but they all agree he was fair, and he was a very successful rancher. Sunnyside was a prosperous, well-kept ranch.

Mother and Daddy in newly fenced yard

Lila resting on baled hay loader

Sunnyside as seen from the 'bench' above the ranch

The ranch house 1950's

Grandpa and Grandma Famie wedding picture

4 *Mother's Birthday Present*

On December 12, 1938, my parents made the sixty-five-mile trip to Ely from Sunnyside for my mother's twenty-seventh birthday. That afternoon at 4:00 p.m., two weeks before I was due, Mom and my aunt Jo decided to take Warner, age seventeen months, for a walk before it was time to go back to the ranch. Halfway through the walk, Mom went into labor. I was born at the Steptoe Valley Hospital in East Ely, but I've always believed my soul was born at Sunnyside. My mother's first question after my birth was, "Is it still my birthday?" She always told me I was the best birthday present she ever had. I arrived early and quickly while she was near a hospital which I think was the first of many times when I tried to make my mother's life easier.

However, I don't think she believed I was such a blessing when Warner and I were babies. She was cooking three meals a day for as many as twenty men during the summer months. She baked three loaves of bread every other day. That meant keeping a fire going in the wood cookstove for the three hours it took for the loaves to bake. It was wonder bread, she once told me, because it was a wonder it didn't burn up. She made butter whenever enough cream had accumulated to fill the churn.

Every morning after the breakfast dishes were done, Ed Rowlie, our hired man, carried a huge stainless steel bowl (much too large to fit into the sink) and all the parts that went with the cream separator into the kitchen. He'd done the milking at four o'clock that morning, then carried the buckets of milk to the milk cellar where he separated the milk from the cream. Mom would then need to refill the sink with hot soapy water. There were twenty-six discs hooked onto a circular metal bar, and each one had to be washed separately and sterilized in the very hot water and then carefully rinsed. The bar was then placed in a large drainer before they were towel dried. Other parts of the separator including a large metal spout and eight other pieces all needed to be washed. When the breakfast dishes were done and the separator was sterilized and taken back to the milk cellar, Mom began preparing for the midday meal. The number of hired men varied, but Ed Rowlie was always on the ranch.

The hardest chore of all was the laundry, and with two babies in diapers it had to be done often. When I was born, my dad bought Mom a washing machine that ran on direct current. That meant she did not have to turn the wringer washer by hand; it could be run by the water-powered generator instead. The washing machine was now located some ways from the house in the powerhouse. She would have to put me in the wagon with the basket of dirty clothes and lead Warner down the path across the creek to do the laundry. It was a challenge to keep Warner out of the oil and grease in the small room and away from the creek.

She'd add soap flakes to the water in the washer then let the whites agitate for a few minutes before feeding each article one piece at a time through the ringer into a washtub of rinse water. Mom sloshed the clothing around with a large paddle until everything was rinsed, and then she'd reverse the wringer and feed the denim jeans, shirts, underwear, socks, towels, dishcloths, tablecloths, bedding, and piles of clean diapers back through the wringer. Finally, she had to put the heavy, damp clothes in the basket and haul them, along with two babies, back to the house where the clotheslines were.

My mother complained very little (mostly because she knew it would do no good), but she never forgot a morning when life just became too much for her. After hanging all the wet clothes on the clotheslines, one line broke and many pieces of clothing fell in the dirt. This was not the first time a line had broken, but whenever she became upset, she got no response. That morning Daddy and Uncle Murray were sipping coffee and visiting when she came through the kitchen door and up the step to the dining room carrying a whole pile of mud-covered clothes and dragging the broken clothesline. She dropped them onto the floor in front of the two men, threw herself on top of the pile, and began to cry hysterically.

Neither man said a word to her. They stood up, put on their hats, and headed out the back door. Shortly afterward my mother heard the powerplant and the cement mixer start, and she heard someone welding down at the shop. Within hours, Uncle Murray and my father had two huge metal pipes, with six-foot cross pipes, welded onto them, cemented in the ground. They stretched heavy wires between the metal pipes and bolted them in place. That clothesline stayed in place for the rest of the years when Mom did laundry at the ranch and is probably still standing today.

One other morning, in the middle of haying season, Mom climbed out of bed, got dressed in her usual housedress, apron, cotton stockings, and comfortable shoes, brushed her hair, and walked to the kitchen where she collapsed on the floor. Hired men were sitting on the back porch, waiting for breakfast. My dad needed to be mowing the hay that day so the men could rake and stack it. Cowboys had come off the range the night before. My brother and I were waking and needing to be fed.

Daddy yelled for Ed Rowlie, our hired man, to come feed the men. Then he helped Mom, who was weak and listless, into the front seat of our new touring car, a 1939 Mercury. He loaded Warner and me in the backseat, and we headed to Ely over the rutted dirt road to the doctor.

"We've done tests on Lila's heart and lungs, but I don't expect to find anything wrong," Dr. Ross told Daddy. "I believe she's overtired to the point of complete physical exhaustion. She needs to go to bed for a week." It had not been too many months since my parents had made another trip to see Dr. Ross.

As a newborn baby, I was crying day and night. Mother would nurse me, but I would continue to cry and neither I nor my mother had slept much for almost two weeks. Dr. Ross checked us both over and announced I was starving to death. Mom's milk had no nutrients—probably because she was so exhausted.

Mom certainly did not get to go to bed for a week after her collapse, but Daddy did begin hiring my older cousins, Evelyn and Zelda, and other young girls from Lund during haying season. Once he hired a girl from the employment agency in Ely. After driving her to the ranch, the girl developed a "sick stomach" and demanded to be taken all the way back to Ely that night. My guess is she looked at the work she was expected to do and wanted no part of it. Daddy's sister, Aunt Jo, and Mother's sister, Aunt Ruth, sometimes came to help out during the summer months until I was old enough to work beside my mother.

By the time I was eight years old, I could help my mother in many ways. I was able to set the table, wash the dishes, dry the cream separator, and churn the butter. I could sweep the floors and straighten the house every morning and dust the living room once a week. I'd drag the coffee table out to the front lawn and dump off the dried manure which had collected during the week from Daddy's boots, and I could climb on top of the player piano and dust it. I ran to the basement where most of the food was stored when my mother needed something. I learned to make desserts which we needed for the noon and evening meals. I liked to make cakes and cookies which, of course, were made with fresh eggs, cream, and butter. I didn't mind helping my mother because that was the only way I could be with her, and I knew how much she needed me.

It was said that my mother was the best cook in the whole area. Her dessert specialties were pies made with hot-water pie crust, ice cream which she froze in ice trays, and her own recipe for sheet cake with cooked icing. She used few recipes because she had to cook using only the available ingredients. Her magic was that she could stretch any meal to accommodate anyone who stopped at the ranch at mealtime. Sunnyside was on what the travelers back then called "the grub line." That was the place where they all timed their dinner and supper stops because they knew they'd always be fed excellent food. She'd see "a dust coming through the gap" and throw more ingredients into the pot. Many times she sat on a chair at the breadboard eating shredded wheat or bread and milk. I believed there wasn't enough food for her, but she never admitted that. She'd just say, "I'm tired of eating my own cooking."

We'll never know whether Mom was sorry they decided to take over a run-down ranch and work themselves almost to death to make it pay. I know she had other dreams that had nothing to do with the ranch. She was in love with a teacher at her high school who supposedly had a heart condition. My grandfather strongly discouraged her from marrying him because she would be burdened with an "invalid" for the rest of her life. He could have had a heart murmur or something as simple as that. She thought about going on a Mormon mission after high school. Her father had forbidden her to do that. She borrowed money from her older sister, Mabel, to go to business school in San Francisco. That was the most memorable year of her life, but Daddy insisted she come home after her first year and marry him.

I remember my mother ordered a set of workbooks based on a popular book *Making Friends and Influencing People* by Dale Carnegie. They had orange hardback covers, and they came on the mail truck on a Tuesday. Mother sent them back when the mail truck returned on Friday. Daddy had seen them and was furious. I always felt my mother wanted more from her life. She made a commitment when she and Daddy took over the ranch, though, and she stuck to it. That is a valuable legacy she left her family.

After the ranch was sold, Mom and Daddy had several years when they were able to travel in their trailer and fish. Mom loved to fish. She told me those years in her fifties were her best years. Warner, Bonnie, and I were married and on our own; they had money to do what they wanted to do; and her health was good. She loved picnics, to be outside and to go for drives to see the autumn leaves and the wild flowers. Her hobby was digging for purple bottles in old dumps.

Mother lived in a townhouse in Las Vegas for twelve years after Daddy died. She had plenty of money and plenty of time to relax. Her favorite television shows were *Perry Mason* and *Gunsmoke*. She read every Louis Lamour book she could find. Mom had three close friends and her sisters to keep her company. Then within four years, her sister, Ruth, and all of her friends died. After that, she was very lonely. "Just keep making new friends throughout your life because they die on you," she told me. She died in 1988 at age seventy-six of emphysema.

Mother with Warner and Sally Jo

Daddy by his new Mercury

Mother's birthday present

5 *Aunt Jo*

My very first memory is of my Aunt Jo. She is rushing out the kitchen door toward me as I am crying. I had awakened to find myself in the backseat of our sedan where it was parked by the creek. I was hot and sweaty and sticking to the wet backseat. Willow branches scraping across the front windshield woke me, and when I realized I was alone, I became scared. Aunt Jo lifted me out of the car and began to calm me. "Sally Jo, you are fine. We are right here. We'll never leave you." She carried me into the kitchen and comforted me before continuing to help my mother put away the month's worth of flour, sugar, canned goods, and other staples they'd bought in Ely.

Aunt Jo, herself, seemed to be one of the staples on the ranch. She was there for Warner and me and for my mother whenever she was needed. Uncle Al worked in a garage in Ely where they lived, and their son, Elwood, stayed on our ranch every summer helping my dad. During the winter, the three of them often came to help out on the weekends. They would get there on Friday nights after I'd gone to bed. I could never go to sleep because I'd be too excited. When Warner and I heard her voice outside our bedroom, we'd jump out of bed and run to her. She'd hug and kiss us and then take us back to our beds, promising we'd have all weekend to be together.

Aunt Jo lost a baby after Elwood was born and apparently couldn't have more children, but she loved children more than anyone I've ever known; she especially loved Warner and me. Aunt Jo didn't endorse the theory that children "were to be seen and not heard." She spent endless amounts of time playing games with us and reading to us. Our needs always came first. She was one of the angels in my life because my mother didn't have much time to spend with me in my early years.

Aunt Jo was also surely an angel in the life of my cousin Lyle. Lyle was the son of Aunt Jo's youngest sister, Phyllis. He developed muscular dystrophy at age six. He was born in 1935 at a time when there were no provisions for the schooling of disabled children. He sat in the tiny front room of his mother's house in East Ely in a wheelchair for ten years until he died at age fifteen. Aunt Jo read book after book to him as his legs shriveled more each year. I remember seeing comic books beside him when we'd go to visit, so I think Aunt Jo might have taught him to read too.

By the time I was in the third grade, Elwood had been drafted in the army, so Aunt Jo offered to come live at Sunnyside and teach Warner and me. She had gone to "Normal School" and was certified to teach. That year I got the red measles. I was kept in my darkened bedroom for two weeks because light would make me go blind. Of course, I couldn't read, and there was no radio or music. That was traumatic for a little girl who was used to living outside. Aunt Jo sat on the other twin bed on the opposite side of the window in my bedroom. Hour after hour she'd slide a book under the blind for light and read to me. She read *The Secret Garden, Little Women,* and *Little Men.* I remember asking her to reread some parts.

No amount of work ever seemed too daunting to Aunt Jo. "We can have these curtains down, washed, ironed, and put back up in an hour," she'd say to my mother. Of course, it ended up being a full-day project, but that didn't stop her from taking on another task. "We'll have it done by supper," she'd say.

Aunt Jo was my favorite of my father's seven sisters when I was young. She was an attractive, physically strong, large-boned woman. As she aged, she had the most beautiful salt-and-pepper hair always perfectly styled. At a time when women wore only dresses, hers were covered with a clean freshly ironed apron most of the time.

When Uncle Murray died, Aunt Jo and Uncle Al leased the Hiko Ranch for five years until Keith, his oldest son, graduated from high school and Aunt Ouida got her teaching certificate. It was fun to stay with Aunt Jo because she'd take us swimming at Ash Springs, a natural hot springs in the valley. I got to know many of the women in Hiko and Alamo. I think being with Aunt Jo helped me learn social skills that I had no opportunity to learn at Sunnyside.

Throughout my life, letters Aunt Jo wrote to me were addressed to Sally Jo which she called me all her life. Aunt Jo had a problem getting names straight, but she always got mine right the first time. She'd call a person five or six names before she'd finally get it right. She called every boy child Warner first, before finally getting the right name. Her grandson named his first and only son, Warner. "We decided we might as well because that's what he'll be called anyway," he told us.

More than once I've made decisions in my life by first asking myself if Aunt Jo would approve. Once I asked my mother whether I should do a certain thing. My mother thought a minute and then answered, "I'm pretty sure God would forgive you, but I'm not sure about your Aunt Jo." Naturally I did not do that certain thing.

I remember going shopping in Paso Robles, California, with Aunt Jo. She and Uncle Al had bought a ranch across from the airport there while visiting Elwood in the army at Ft. Bragg. She held my hand as we walked even though I was in college by then. To her, I was still little Sally Jo, and to me, she was still one of the most wonderful, powerful people in my life.

She was in her eighties when she got ovarian cancer. She was able to stay in her home on the ranch with the help of a loving daughter-in-law and many grandchildren. I went to see her shortly before she died. She was as excited as a child as we sat together, holding hands on her sofa and watching the television. She seemed relaxed, taking a temporary break from her fight with cancer. "I look forward to the *Lawrence Welk Show* every week, Sally Jo," she told me. She died a few weeks later in October of 1988, just five months after my mother's death.

Aunt Jo (third from left) with her sisters

Elwood, Warner, Al, Sally Jo and Aunt Jo

6 Ed Rowlie

I can't remember when Ed wasn't on the ranch. To me, he was the ranch. He milked the cows (they usually gave very little milk while Ed was away), irrigated, mended fences and painted gates, chopped wood, and crept into our house each morning to build a fire in the stoves and make the coffee. He was never given the title of foreman, but because he had been with us so long, he came to believe that he was in charge second only to my father. He made life miserable for the hired men who had to share the bunkhouse with him, causing many of them to draw their pay and ask to be taken back to town.

The bunkhouse was a small room with one small window and one small door. Ed's cot was in the corner next to the potbellied stove. Pictures of his two beautiful daughters, who looked like models to me, were on a small desk next to the front door. I don't think they ever wrote or came to visit him. Once a week, he'd bring in the washtub, which hung on the outside of the bunkhouse, fill it with water he heated on his stove, and bathe. He tried to keep his little house neat and clean, but the hired men he had to share his space with threw their sleeping bags and clothes on the army cots along the back wall. Some of them were grimy, toothless winos with atrocious manners who did not bother to bathe or change their clothes. We didn't have to live with them, but they ate every meal with us, and that was bad enough.

One man my dad hired would come into the kitchen when we rang the dinner bell, spear a chunk of meat with the first fork he could reach, and carry it around to his plate. Then he'd lift the meat to his mouth with the fork and use his knife to cut a bite off close to his mouth as the rest of the meat fell onto his plate. Another man told about killing and eating chickens without cleaning them. "They're already stuffed," he told us. "Why clean them out and stuff them again?" Many times we'd lose our appetites just listening to and watching these men. Ed would butt into their conversations so often that many of them quit telling their boring stories. The trouble was Ed's stories were equally as boring. If he ever learned any piece of information, he'd hang around outside the kitchen door until my mother finally stepped outside. "I need to go listen to his story," she'd say, "because he won't leave until I do." His news was usually something about an animal or a new project he'd finished, but sometimes it was really exciting news when someone stopped by from the "outside world."

I couldn't figure out when Ed slept. He would be sitting on the small cement stoop in front of the bunkhouse when I climbed into my bedroll at night, and he'd wake me up whistling all the way to the barn to milk the cows at four o'clock each morning. He whistled when he came back to the milk cellar and separated the cream from the milk, rinsed the manure off the bottom of the large separator bowl in the creek, and took it and all the many parts into the kitchen so Mom and I could wash and sterilize them. We always knew where Ed was by listening for his whistle.

One of my earliest memories happened late one night when Ed woke Warner and me. He held Warner's hand and carried me up the sidewalk to the open yard above the ranch. There we saw what seemed like every star in the sky falling. I was about three years old, but I have never forgotten the wonder of that sight. Since there were no other visible lights—not even a flashlight anywhere in the world, the meteor shower was even more spectacular. Ed knew this was an experience we'd never forget. I've seen only one other such phenomenon in my lifetime.

Once a year, Ed would take what pay was owed to him by my father, find a ride to town, and spend his entire vacation drunk. Daddy would send Mom to town after about a week to find Ed and bring him home. A few times I went along to help her search the many bars in Ely. After his binges, he'd come home with a haircut, new Levi's (rolled up at the bottom because Ed was a small man), a new shirt, and sometimes a new pair of work boots or a new Levi jacket. There would always be a toy or something for Warner and me.

Unlike my father who rode off to the range on horseback for days at a time, Ed was always at the ranch (except for his yearly binges) and was there if ever we needed anything. He was there the day Warner fell on a broken whiskey bottle while we were playing in the creek behind the house. Warner stood up on the narrow wooden bridge with blood shooting out of his leg like a powerful faucet just as Ed walked around the corner of the house. Ed yelled for my mother who came rushing out of the kitchen door.

"We need a tourniquet," he told her. By now he had Warner laying on the cement porch and was pinching his thigh to stop the bleeding. Mom grabbed a dish towel, and together they tied off the artery and placed pillows for Warner to lay on. That particular day, my father had taken our Mercury out to the white sage flats to check on the water troughs. Ed rushed to the saddle house, saddled old Brownie, an old, slow horse we used to bring in the other horses from the pasture, and headed out to find Daddy. It was a six-mile ride, but the old horse made it "in good time" as my grandfather always said. Daddy rushed home, loaded us in the car, and headed to Ely. On the way we passed Ed riding slowly home on old Brownie. Warner was calm through the whole incident, but I cried from the moment he began to bleed until we got him to Ely where he got sixty stitches in his little six-year-old leg.

Ed was again the only man on the place the day he decided to burn the cheat grass from under Mom's clotheslines. As he burned little patches, he would put the fire out with water from a bucket he had nearby. Suddenly a gust of wind came up and the fire got out of control. Ed began to scream for my mother who sent me to get Elva, a hired man's wife who lived in the other little house on our ranch. She was the only other adult on the ranch that day. Within minutes, the fence was on fire, then the orchard, then it was heading to the powerhouse, and finally the slaughter pen and the corrals. My mother, Elva, Warner, and I began dipping gunny sacks in the ditch and beating the fire in between carrying and dumping buckets of water. Fortunately the wind died down, and the fire stayed below the house. At some point we realized it was out and that we had kept it from reaching the corrals and the animals, but Ed was covered with water and soot, and his shirt was badly ripped. He was so exhausted that Mom and Elva needed to help him to the bunkhouse. We had all worked hard, but Warner and I were children and Mom and Elva weren't as strong as men, so Ed had really been the one who saved the ranch. We thought it would be a few days before Ed could work again, but at four o'clock the next morning Ed was up, as usual, whistling from the bunkhouse to the barn.

I was too young to remember another situation Ed dealt with, but I've heard the story from my cousin, Guy, who was there. A calf fell through the rotted timber that had covered the fifty-or sixty-year-old cesspool below our house. Without hesitation, Ed tied a rope around his waist and instructed Guy to hold onto the end of the rope while he jumped in to rescue the calf. He saved the calf, and then after soaking and scrubbing in his washtub filled with scalding water, he built a new top on the cesspool that would last forever.

I remember the day I was happily running in the yard when Ed opened the gate by the granary and called for me to get Mom. All the skin was off the front of his body, and it was slick and blue, and all of his veins were showing like a rabbit I'd once seen my father skin. He told us he had stepped off the back of the tractor and put the clutch in neutral, but it slipped out. The large tractor wheel began backing over him. I'm not sure how he got out from under the tire or how he managed to walk clear from the field to the house before he collapsed. Fortunately the car was at the ranch that day, and we got him to the hospital in Ely. I think we stayed in town for a few days because I remember seeing him laying in the hospital bed. We brought him back to his bunkhouse as soon as he was able to move. Before long, we heard his familiar whistling as he headed to the barn to do the morning chores.

I had learned how to do many jobs around the ranch, so when I was about eleven, my mother decided I could do the cooking when she needed to go to Ely. The men would hang around on the back porch, peeking in the back screen door if the meals were not on time—6:00 a.m., 12:00 noon, and 6:00 p.m. My biggest problem was getting everything done at the same time. I knew how to do a roast and potatoes, but my gravy was almost inedible. One day Ed came into the kitchen. "You got some learnin' to do on yer gravy," he said. "Them men ain't even able to eat it." He asked me to show him how I was making gravy. I was scraping all the good brown drippings from the roast into the sink and then thickening the grease. Once he explained that I needed to dump out the grease, then add water to the brown drippings, my gravy improved considerably.

Often when Mom went to town, I would do the ironing to surprise her. Ironing was a hot job in the summer because we had to build a huge fire in the cookstove and heat stove irons. We had two so that one could be heating while we used the other one. My mother ironed shirts, dresses, aprons, handkerchiefs, and tablecloths. I loved to see the smile on my mother's face when she got home to find her ironing all done. Ed showed me how to iron shirts—starting with the collar and sleeves—and handkerchiefs by folding them in half, pressing them, folding them into a quarter, and pressing them again. If I ever have the occasion to iron a handkerchief again, I won't have forgotten that skill.

Ed always spoiled Warner and me. My dad refused to buy me a new nine-volt battery when I'd fall asleep listening to my radio and the battery would go dead. Ed would hear me begging my dad, so he'd slip the next person who went to town (usually my mother) some money to get me another battery. He would have Mom buy me plants and seeds when she went to town too because my next favorite thing after music was plants. He always wanted Mom to get Warner and me something special for Christmas.

I received a phone call from my father while I was going to University of Nevada in Reno in 1958. "Ed has tuberculosis. We are bringing him to the sanitarium near Reno." This was good news and bad news. He was very ill with a hole in his lung "the size of an orange," but I would get to visit him. Every Sunday, Aunt Caroline and I would bake something and drive the ten miles to Steamboat Springs, where the sanitarium was, to visit Ed. She would wait in the car while I went in to visit because she was afraid she would catch tuberculosis. He finally recovered and returned to the ranch.

I carefully unfolded the last gift Ed ever gave me and placed it on my Thanksgiving table as I do every year. It was the wedding gift he gave me in 1959.

"Buy the biggest linen tablecloth you cin find," Ed said to my mother as she was leaving for Ely one morning. "Don't never mind the money; it ain't no concern to me."

It was an ecru damask linen tablecloth large enough for a banquet table. I have used it over and over in my lifetime as I have used the information and nurturing that Ed gave me throughout my young life. My father sold the ranch in 1962, selling with it Ed's soul, I believe. He died a short time later at his son's home in Utah.

Ed Rowlie on Brownie

Ed with Jimmy the steer

Ed Rowlie

7 *The Clock Strikes Four*

Out on the ranch, the Christmas season began for my brother and me when the *Sears Roebuck and Montgomery Wards* Christmas catalogs arrived on the mail truck. We poured over every page of the toy sections until the catalog fell apart. I eventually had to decide on one doll for Santa Claus to bring me, and Warner chose a truck. Looking back, I think it was a miracle that Santa found us out on that isolated cattle ranch in Nevada, but I remember the Christmas Eve of 1944, when he actually came twice.

After our supper, my parents and Warner and I sat in the living room near the oil stove, sipping hot chocolate and looking in wonder at our beautiful tree. We had decorated it after cutting it down and bringing it home from the hills above the ranch. We sang Christmas songs while Mom played the player piano. The words were printed on each roll as the paper slowly moved around the cylinder. My dad played "Silent Night" on his harmonica, and then since Warner and I knew Santa would not come while we were up, we announced we were going to bed early. Cookies and milk were set out for Santa; Dad turned off the powerplant, and the ranch became dark and quiet—except for the chimes of the clock on the small shelf in the dining room outside our bedroom door.

"When the clock chimes four times," my mother told us, "you can wake us up, and we'll all go into the living room and see what Santa has left for you."

It was impossible for Warner and me to get to sleep, so we began to count the chimes each quarter hour and then the dongs on the hour . . . nine, ten, finally one, two. We would whisper the number to each other every hour to make sure we'd counted right. At three o'clock Warner decided we should take our flashlight and creep into the living room and just look at our toys, but we wouldn't touch them.

It was very dark, but as the flash of light moved under the tree, I saw my beautiful doll. She was leaning against a package, and she was even more beautiful than she had looked in the catalog. We sat by the tree, shivering and moving the flashlight from my doll to Warner's blue truck. Then we crept back into our beds and again began listening to the clock. We counted each chime and finally the dongs . . . one, two, three, four. Four o'clock! We threw off our covers, grabbed our robes and slippers, and rushed to our parents' bedroom.

My father quickly dressed and went down to turn the powerplant on again. Mom, Warner, and I went into the living room to wait for the lights to come on. Then Warner and I looked at each other in total amazement. There setting next to Warner's truck was a General MacArthur doll. And setting next to my doll was a second truck, just like Warner's, but it was red. Of course Santa knew we always played with our toys together. I had always wished for the same toy Warner got, but I wouldn't give up my doll either. This was the perfect solution, but why did he wait until early on Christmas morning to come back with a doll for Warner and a truck for me? To ask our parents about this would be to admit we had sneaked out of our beds before the clock chimed four. Maybe Santa just had two extra toys, we decided.

That player piano is in my living room today, and the old clock sets on top of it. I usually forget to keep it wound most of the year, but every Christmas Eve I wind it and listen to the chimes—*one, two, three, four* . . .

I don't remember asking how the "second Christmas" came about, but I have an answer that makes sense. Mom had probably bought the General MacArthur doll for Warner. She knew Daddy would disapprove of Warner getting a doll, so she sneaked in with his doll and the truck after they had set up the first two toys from Santa and before we got up. I would get a truck, so each of us would get two things from Santa. She probably thought Daddy would not get as upset seeing Warner's doll under the tree on Christmas morning. Daddy loved Christmas.

Sally and Warner with Charles McArthur doll

8 *Warner and Sourdough*

For the first ten years of my life, my brother Warner was my only playmate, my caretaker, and the most important person in my life. I was a little over a year old when Warner loaded me into his red wagon and pulled me as far away from the house as he could. He dumped me out into the dirt and took the empty wagon home. My mother panicked. "Where is Sally Jo? You were supposed to watch out for her."

Warner pointed toward the road. He let her know he was tired of carrying me or pulling me around. "Sourdough needs to learn to walk," he told Mom in his baby talk. Warner did not talk very well, so for quite a while my name, Sally Jo, sounded like Sourdough. That was what I was called for a few years by the hired men and my cousins on the ranch.

I was making my way home when they found me, but I was not walking. I was happily crawling up the middle of the dirt road, stopping to eat dirt along the way. I don't remember, but I probably believed, even then, that if Warner left me in the road, that was where I was supposed to be. My brother was my hero.

"When you wake up from your nap, Sally Jo, there will be a surprise for you," my mother told me one afternoon. The surprise was coming around the corner of the fence above the front yard just as I came out the front door about an hour later. Daddy and Ed Rowlie were dragging a small shed on log skids hooked to the tractor with a chain. It was a deserted building from when the CCC Camp was stationed below the ranch. The Civilian Conservation Corps was part of the new deal initiated by President Roosevelt in the 1930s. Thousands of unemployed young men were recruited to battle against destruction and erosion of our natural resources. While they lived in the camp a mile below the ranch, they improved the springs and built wells on the government range where we ran our cattle. They also built us a beautiful eight-foot-long dining table with two benches.

I soon realized the weathered old shed was to be Warner's and my playhouse. My dad and Ed situated it in a level place next to the creek, and Warner, Ed, and I immediately went to work. We found an old chunk of linoleum in the store room, and Ed cut it to fit our floor with sheep shears. Ed found us some paint and two brushes, and we painted the house inside and out. I can only imagine the mess a four- and five-year-old must have made with that paint. Ed certainly did most of the actual painting.

Then we began moving in. Our household possessions consisted of a wooden cupboard with glass doors my grandma had made for me, doll bunk beds that Ed had built, a table and chairs, a small tin sink with a tray in the back to put water in so the faucet actually worked, a rocking chair, toy dishes, trunks, dolls, and doll clothes. I had one doll from each Christmas since I was two years old. I remember Mary, my rag doll, a baby doll named Charlotte, Warner's General MacArthur doll, and my last two dolls, Irene and Zelda.

Warner began digging postholes and building a corral for our stick horses and rock cows. He built a slaughter pen with a block and tackle like Daddy's and a loading chute. Many of our rock cows were on "open range" which meant they were all over the ranch. Warner's cows were branded with a brown crayon, mine with a purple one. One day Mom and I were walking along the creek when we heard, then saw a coiled up rattlesnake. Mom picked up a huge rock and dropped it on the snake's head. I began to howl. The snake-killing rock was my prize bull. Couldn't she see the purple brand on it?

Warner built a cover over our wagon by bending pieces of lathe and covering them with canvas, so it looked like Daddy's sheep wagon. Sometimes we would have to go on a roundup where we'd pull our "sheep wagon" all over the ranch loading up branded cows. I rode my stick horse along beside him and led his horse by the twine around his stick-shaped head. When Warner pulled the wagon back to the corral, I helped him unload our brown and purple rock cows into the corral. Later some would be put in the loading chute and moved to another part of our "ranch." Roads, troughs, wells, and signs we made could be found throughout the sagebrush all over our ranch.

When we got hungry, I'd go back to the playhouse and set dishes on the table so we could have our lunch. Our meal consisted of peanut butter and jelly sandwiches and Vienna sausages that Mom had prepared for us. Mom usually did not see us from breakfast until afternoon when we were supposed to come home and take a rest, but Ed always seemed to be around somewhere watching out for us.

As Warner got a little older, he built an upstairs in our house by pounding rafters across the ceiling and putting sheets of plywood up there. He put slats up the wall for a ladder so we could get to our new addition. I stored all the blankets, doll clothes, and dolls up there.

Next Warner built a garage off the side of our house and covered it with tar paper, so we'd have a place to keep our wagon and tricycles. Then Ed dumped cement in the wheelbarrow. We added water and began mixing with our shovels. This became our front step when we dumped it onto the ground in front of the door. I dug up a bit of dirt beside the house and planted flower seeds. Our home was now perfect.

We played in this playhouse until we were seven or eight. That was when Warner decided he was too old to play that game. I remember seeing that coming one day when we were calling from one side of the ranch to the other as we played, and Ed said something like, "I didn't know boys played with dolls." Shortly after that, Warner dug a hole and buried his General MacArthur doll. It never was as much fun to play in my playhouse without Warner. Fortunately, we had other games to play though.

I got a doll and accessories every Christmas from Santa, but it was a given that he always gave me exactly what Warner got too. I guess after listening to me pitch fits the first few Christmases of our lives, Santa just gave up and bought two trucks, two tractors, two farm animal sets, and two guns or whatever else Warner asked for.

After Warner stopped playing in the playhouse with me, we found a more acceptable activity for a boy. Warner and I built a farm where we played with our trucks and tractors and farm animals in a fenced-off area where Daddy grew strawberries at one time. Log Cabin syrup cans became our ranch houses. Each time Aunt Jo stopped by Sunnyside on her way to Ely from Hiko, she'd pick up our ration books, which we needed during the war to buy sugar and gasoline among other things. She'd ask what we wanted her to bring us. Warner and I always asked for Log Cabin syrup. I'm sure she knew we were more interested in the cans than the syrup.

We built picket fence corrals on our farm with gates that opened and closed. We dug a reservoir at the bottom of our farm then ran lead pipe to the top. We'd put the garden hose into the top end of the pipe and let the water drip down the pipe until our reservoir was full. We planted twigs around the house and reservoir but soon realized that without roots, they died. Warner built plows and harrows and mowers and rakes out of tin and lathe which he hooked onto the tractors. He made two windmills from lathe and tin. He built barns and sheds and fences from old lumber, and we painted them tractor orange with paint we found in the shop. Our cattle were the stink bugs that we located as we walked the "open range." We'd back our trucks up to a particular stink bug who immediately put his butt in the air and began to stink as we gently prodded him up a ramp we had build until he got into the back of the truck. Then we'd close the tailgate so he would not escape and drive off to the ranch, where we'd unload him into the corral with other stink bugs we'd rounded up and carefully close the gate.

At about ages seven or eight, Daddy decided we were old enough to work beside him and Mother to help make Sunnyside Ranch a success. Warner and I were no longer allowed to be two children playing all day with no cares in the world. We went to work.

But during those early years of our lives, we were allowed to play, and play we did—riding through the brush on our stick horses, running in the creek, and playing in our playhouse and farm for hours and hours without interruption. My aunts and cousins told us we surely had the most perfect childhoods they ever knew any children to have. I think they were mostly right.

Warner with the farm we built

Warner and Sally on stump by playhouse

Warner pulling Sally Jo in his wagon

9 One of the Last Real Cowboys

Aunt Jo brought Kathryn and Kent up from Hiko to stay at Sunnyside with us while Mom and Daddy went to the Caliente Hospital. We were told, "Your Uncle Murray has taken a turn for the worse." It was the middle of the night when I heard the hushed voices outside my bedroom door. I pretended I was asleep when Mom tiptoed into the room to check on me and my four-year-old cousin. She stood by Kathryn Rose's bed and kissed her on the forehead before she touched my hair and left the room. I now realize she must have been wondering how she would attend to the horrific task that awaited her the next morning.

Early the following morning, my mother came back into our bedroom as Kathryn Rose and I were climbing out of bed and pulling on our boots. She suggested that we take a short walk before breakfast. My father had gone to find Warner and Kathryn's brothers, Keith and Kent, who were sleeping on cots in the front yard. As we walked along the creek just below the house, Mother quietly said, "Kathryn Rose, your daddy died last night."

Kathryn didn't understand. "Will we put him in a matchbox and bury him like we do the baby chickens?" she asked. I was two years older than Kathryn, and I understood about death. My cats and my dog, Shiner, and my baby lamb had died. Death meant sadness, and it was final.

Everyone in my world and even the ranch itself seemed to mourn for Uncle Murray's death for months and even years. His death seemed to suck the spirit out of our entire family. My father lost his best friend and the one person who could keep him centered and controlled. He never got over his older brother's death.

I can still picture Uncle Murray sitting in the oak chair by the desk in our dining room at Sunnyside, his hat propped on his knee, he and Daddy telling stories and joking. He usually had his fiddle with him. Murray was a gifted musician. He played the fiddle, mandolin, and banjo. Once he ordered a mandolin out of a catalog. It came on the mail truck on a Tuesday, and by the following Saturday night he'd learned it well enough to play it at the church dance in Lund. The last memory I have of Uncle Murray is of him sitting in that oak chair with his right arm bandaged to the elbow, his arm in a sling.

I remember hearing about the accident at Cold Springs. Keith, age twelve, was with his father when it happened. What he remembers is a large thunder cloud enveloping the cowboys as they were branding. Everyone seemed paralyzed for a second or more, and what transpired in the next few seconds seemed to be happening in slow motion. Murray had thrown the lasso at a calf, but his horse's front feet got caught in the rope, and he began to buck. No horse could buck Murray off, but as the horse overran the calf, Murray's fingers got caught in the loop. He watched his thumb and two fingers fly by as they were ripped from his hand. The cloud lifted, and the cowboys rushed to help Murray. They got him off his horse and placed his blood-soaked hand in a washbasin and poured horse iodine over it. The pain was excruciating. They then put him in John Wright's new car, and Kay Wright and George Nesbitt took off for Caliente to the doctor.

Keith, Jay, and John Wright stayed behind to feed the horses and do what chores needed to be done before returning to Hiko. As the three of them were driving into Hiko about three hours later, they met George, Kay, and Aunt Ouida just leaving with Murray in his car taking him to Caliente. Apparently John's new car had developed a clogged fuel line, and they had to make the trip from Coal Valley to Hiko going twenty miles per hour. They had just arrived at Hiko, picked up Ouida and Murray's car, and were heading to the doctor. Murray stayed in the hospital for three days. When he came home from the hospital, he held his bandaged right hand in front of Aunt Ouida and announced, "This is the end of Murray Whipple."

Keith didn't see his father again for a week. He was back at Murphy Meadows when Murray came walking toward him with his right arm bandaged and in a sling. He sat down beside Keith and began talking to him. He asked if Keith had remembered the thunder cloud on the day of the accident. He told Keith that there were voices in that cloud that said to him, "Your time is up, and you need to get your house in order." Murray related the same story to Dan Stewart. He told Keith to go on with his life and to be good at whatever he did and to stay with the cattle and get them to the summer range at Long Water. Keith had had a dream prior to the accident when he was told that he had to lose one of his parents, and he was to choose which one. Of course, he couldn't do that.

Aunt Ouida took Murray to Caliente to get the dressing changed several times after the accident, and his condition was not thought to be serious until he got blood poisoning, and she took him back to the hospital. He developed pleurisy and pneumonia. It seemed he lost his will to live. Mom and Daddy left for Caliente immediately. He died shortly after they arrived at the hospital, one month to the day after losing his fingers; he was fifty years old. Keith did as his father told him and got the cattle to the summer range. He made it back to Sunnyside the same night his father died.

Murray knew his life as a cowboy was over when he lost his fingers. I believe our spirits can die before our bodies. Murray's spirit died that afternoon of June 15, 1945, at Cold Springs. There really isn't much for disabled cowboys to do, and the same scenario replayed many years later when my father's body outlived his spirit.

After his death, Keith, Kent, and Kathryn Rose returned to Hiko to be with their mother. Kathryn Rose was immediately sent across the road to stay with a family friend and was not allowed to come home until after the funeral. She remembers no sadness about the death of her father only that she could not go back home with her mother and brothers. Through a window, she watched people come and go and thought she was being punished for something she didn't know about. It was determined that at four years old she was too young to go to her daddy's funeral. Kent and I were allowed to go. We were six.

On the day of the funeral, a continuous cloud of dust poured from the gap where cars coming up the wash from Hiko and Alamo were first visible from Sunnyside. Almost everybody in Pahranagat Valley and White River Valley attended the funeral. It was one of largest ever held in Lund. He was buried in the Lund cemetery where his mother and a sister were buried and where most of his family would be buried in later years. The engraving on his headstone reads, Murray John Whipple—August 26,1894–July 15, 1945. "A man who never had an enemy."

If Kathryn had gone to her dad's funeral, she would have seen him in what looked to me like a large version of a matchbox lined with blue satin. His coffin was in Uncle Vern's dining room in Lund. When I saw him laying there dressed in a black suit, white shirt, and tie, I thought he looked exactly like my dad; and I began to cry because I thought maybe it was really my dad who had died and everyone was crying for him.

The two brothers did look alike, but they were not alike in other ways. My dad was fun-loving and compassionate, but he had a short-temper and a mean disposition at times. He was a very hardworking, driven man who was determined to make something of himself. Murray was always happy-go-lucky and easygoing. He once wrestled Daddy to the ground to keep him from "beating some sense" into a newly hired cowhand who was not doing his job.

Uncle Murray was the firstborn of ten children who had been raised at Sunnyside. He lived there until he was in his forties when he moved his family seventy-five miles south to Hiko. Murray was the favorite of everyone in the family. He teased his seven sisters unmercifully and gave each of them nicknames that stayed with them all their lives. He went to Ely often to party. A few times he didn't make it home before morning because he'd crash his Mercury coming down Murry summit from Ely. Grandpa, my father, and a brother-in-law or two would go bring him home. As he sat at the breakfast table nursing a hangover, Grandma always assured everyone, "Murray must have eaten bad food at the Crystal Café again."

Uncle Murray was a cowboy, and that is all he ever wanted to be. He is remembered as one of last true bronc busters of Eastern Nevada and the greatest roper in three counties. He roped and broke broncs on the ranch, on the range, and at rodeos. He believed that if horses threw their riders, they became outlaws. It was important to never be bucked off a horse he was breaking. He could take the wildest, meanest horse and patiently break it and train it to become a great roping or cutting horse. One cowboy sat dozing on a cutting horse Murray had trained. Someone quietly slipped off the horse's bridle, and the horse went right on cutting calves and working cows. He was well known in the rodeo circuit all over Eastern Nevada as well.

Once he broke his leg while riding a wild horse out on the range. By the time he got back to the ranch with the rest of the cowboys, his leg was so swollen; they needed to cut his boot and pant leg off. First they had to get him off his horse. Somebody got the idea of lassoing him then kicking the horse out from under him. The idea worked as he dismounted rapidly. Then my father and grandfather straightened his leg and strapped a one-by-four along each side of it. He never went to a doctor. In fact, Murray had never seen a doctor until the accident at Coal Springs even though an autopsy showed that every rib in his body, plus other bones, had been broken at some time in his life.

He married late and lived hard. Murray was twenty-eight when he married Louise (Ouida) Jones who came from Genoa, Nevada, to teach on the ranch. She taught my father and his younger sisters. Murray and Ouida lived in a small bunkhouse at Sunnyside for twelve years. He refused to lease the ranch from Grandpa because he knew how much work would be involved to make it successful. When my parents leased Sunnyside, Murray and Ouida bought the Hiko Ranch. There was no indoor plumbing at Hiko when Murray moved his family there, and he never made any improvements. His passion was only for cowboying.

One story pretty much tells Murray's philosophy of life. A man from the Pahranagat Valley stole some of Murray's hay one night, and a neighbor told Murray who the thief was.

"Well," Murray said, "I need to do more for that fellow if he needs hay that desperately." He never confronted the man nor did he try to get his hay back.

Murray Whipple is still a legend in Eastern Nevada. He lived a short life, but few men represented the lifestyle and philosophy of the true old western cowboy like he did.

Uncle Murray

Murray with two little cowgirls, Sally Jo and Kathryn Rose

Murray John Whipple, the last cowboy

10   *The Wooden Truck*

The wooden truck was about two inches long and had moving wooden wheels. It was laying in front of me on the front porch when I picked it up and hurled it at my father. I aimed for and hit him on his left temple. The world stood still for a moment, our eyes met, and I knew I would be getting the "willowing" of my life. I didn't even run; I just waited for my dad to trim the willow from a tree near the creek. I can still feel the intense stinging and pain across the back of my bare legs, but the incident that triggered my anger and caused me to pick up the truck is even more vivid in my memory.

Warner was dressed in a suit, white shirt, tie, dress shoes, and a dress hat for our special day. This was the suit bought for Warner when we took a trip to Deming, New Mexico, to visit my father's older sister, Leone (Sis). I was wearing a red silk pinafore and white silk blouse Mother had made for me to wear to my cousin Elwood's graduation in Ely. We were all dressed in our best town clothes for a rare trip to Ely. I remember how handsome Warner looked and how proud I was of him. Warner and Daddy were a few steps out the front door ahead of me. Just as I stepped out, I saw my dad turn on the faucet and aim the garden hose with the full stream of water straight at Warner who stood there shocked. Everything he had on was soaking wet, and he began to cry. My mother rushed out. "Whatever possessed you to do such a thing?" she yelled at my father. Then she told Warner to go see what else he could find to wear. Warner would not be going to town in his wonderful suit. He didn't even have another decent outfit to change into. In fact, Warner would not be wearing his suit ever again. My reaction was instantaneous as I reached for the wooden truck.

Nobody could explain to me why Daddy had such a bad temper and was sometimes very mean. Mom's question to Daddy about what "possessed" him to soak Warner was a good one. He did seem to be possessed with some demons he never dealt with. I've listened to stories about his young life, and I believe Grandpa and the family dynamics had a lot to do with my father's anger. Murray was the first born of JL's family. JL favored him from the time of his birth, and Murray became his best friend and confidant. Laverne, the second child, went off to the war, married, and bought a farm in Lund. His third child was his first daughter, Dent. She was always Grandpa's favorite daughter with her long golden ringlets. (It is interesting that Murray and Dent were the only children in the family who died while Grandpa was still alive.) Five more girls were born before there was another son—Clair, my father.

While Murray and Laverne (who were fourteen and twelve years older than my dad) were out with Grandpa, Clair spent most of his time with his dog, reading his favorite books, drawing and hanging out with his older sisters. In school, he excelled in math. Music was his greatest love throughout his life. He was very close to his mother and got his singing voice from her. He played the harmonica and learned to play the accordion later in his life. His five sisters spoiled him. They began calling him Little Punk, and the name Punk stuck with him throughout his life. Grandpa saw him as a spoiled boy and paid little attention to him even though my dad yearned to be with his father.

Fortunately Murray cared about my dad and became the role model and mentor he desperately needed. Murray told of helping my dad out of his bedroll each morning after a long day in the saddle. He was just a young boy, but he'd need Murray to stand him up and get his legs moving. This story tells me that my father suffered from some form of arthritis from a very early age. It probably irritated my grandfather that his young son had a physical problem of some kind.

I hated the other part of my dad's personality as much as his anger. He'd stop talking to anyone for a week or two. We never knew why, but I'd always think I must have done something wrong. His personality was so strong that it seemed like a dark cloud hung over the entire ranch when he was in one of his miserable moods. It usually took someone who stopped by from off the ranch to get Daddy talking and laughing. He would greet them, and soon he'd be fine again.

In the 1940s and '50s, not much was known about mental illness, but looking back it would seem he suffered from some form of manic depression. What we called "his moods" were bouts of depression. His way of managing them was to work. During one particular bad time in my life, I told my dad I thought I needed to see a psychiatrist because I was really depressed. "That is not necessary," Daddy told me. "Just go down below your house and start digging a trench. Dig until you get to the end of your property, then start filling it back in. That's all you need to do to start feeling better." I have lived most of my life using his "trench theory."

Until Daddy sold the ranch, his "trench theory" worked well for him. There is no doubt that he became a very successful rancher. In the 1950s, he was one of three men appointed by Ezra Taft Benson to be a member of the Nevada Agriculture and Stabilization and Conservation (ASC) Committee. "The ASC Committee played a vital role in state farm and ranch activities," Senator George W. Malone stated when he announced the appointment. He went on to say, "Clair Whipple is an outstanding White Pine County rancher. Members of the committee were selected by the secretary of agriculture because of their outstanding farming and community leadership records." Daddy served on that committee until he sold the ranch.

As he got older and more physically disabled, he could no longer work or even ride a horse. In cowboy terms: "He and Diamond needed to be put out to pasture." He sold the ranch when he was fifty-four. As part of the sale, my parents traded the cattle for a high-end apartment complex near Camelback Mountain in Phoenix, Arizona. They moved to Phoenix to manage the apartments for a short time then moved to Las Vegas. He got valley fever, had a heart attack, and along with the pain of the arthritis he had in his hips, he was miserable. He did have one hip replacement in the 1970s which did not work well, so he refused to have the other hip replaced. He turned to whiskey to ease the pain of his aching, broken body. All of his youth and vitality was gone. All but the memory of his days of riding on the open range and working to make the ranch a success were gone. He never found anything to replace the cowboy life. He was sixty-eight years old when he took his own life on September 20, 1976.

My father was a complex man. He educated himself by surrounding himself with business leaders and people he respected. He had wanted to go to law school with his high school friend, Dutch Horton, but he had no high school diploma. He did not see himself as a blue collar but a professional. He counted on white collar, successful people to be his friends, and because of his dynamic personality and his exceptional good looks, he became their leader. He loved to write but always kept a dictionary and thesaurus next to him because of his limited vocabulary. He was the spokesperson for the ranchers in the area as he was also a gifted speaker. He was asked to entertain at many functions in Lund by singing, reciting poems and readings he'd memorize.

A speaker at his funeral summed up my father. "Clair Whipple might not have been the most loved man, but he was respected by all. He was honest in all his dealings, and 'his word was gold.'" One friend once commented, "As Punk Whipple goes, so goes the world."

Daddy had no use for lazy people. They, according to him, would "never amount to anything." Most were "worthless, no good knotheads!" I was never to show any interest in a kid that croused around. Crousing was bad (whatever that was). His belief was that I could only date someone I would consider marrying. He told me that is what his parents believed too.

I believe the cowboy culture taught to my children by my father has made them the wonderful people they are today. *Any job, no matter how simple, should be done well. Always keep an eye open to see what needs to be done without having to be told. Work on your own time if necessary.* There are more of my dad's great words of wisdom my kids and I have lived by. *The only thing you can't ever get back is your good reputation. You should always wear your spurs; you never know when you might find a horse. It is better to keep your mouth shut and appear stupid than to open it and prove it.*

Because I was a single mom, my kids spent valuable time with my parents. Daddy was the father they needed. They remember camping, fishing, cooking over a fire in Dutch ovens, listening to classic country music on the eight-track tape player in their camp trailer, playing cards, and memorizing words to songs and singing together.

I had a father who loved me and supported me through every trial in my life. The wonderful memories of growing up on the ranch, surrounded by love and joy, far outweigh the occasional dark side of my father. I have many more memories of a vibrant, fun, loving father than a violent, moody one.

Warner in New Mexico wearing his new suit

Daddy with Molly and pups

11 Best Friends on the Ranch

From a donkey to lambs, to cats (I once had thirty-six, all named) to dogs, a steer, horses, and even Maggie, my pet hen—my friends on the ranch were the animals. They were what kept me from being lonely.

One of the first animals I remember was Bette, our pack mule. She was on the ranch before I was born. I started riding her when I was about two. When the cowboys got ready for the roundups, the first thing my dad did was pack old Bette. She never had to be led but followed along behind the cowboys with bedrolls, pans, a coffeepot, and the grub tied on her back. As she got older, she'd not make it to the stopping place until almost dark. The cowboys had to wait for her to arrive before they could eat or even make camp, but they knew she'd always make it. Nobody could make Bette go any faster or in any direction she did not want to go. She was stubborn as a mule.

Our first dog, Shiner, was also on the ranch before I was born. Shiner was a white sheepdog with a black circle around one eye. He was Daddy's dog and helped him work the cattle. My dad told the story about a time when he was out riding and was called back to Sunnyside from the Hagerty Ranch. He left his saddle and Shiner behind and drove home. The other cowboys could not get Shiner to follow them. After several days they rode back to give him food and water; he'd not left my dad's saddle and still would not leave until Daddy returned.

Ed Rowlie made a harness for Shiner once and then hooked him onto our wagon. Warner and I would get in the wagon and yell, "Giddy up!" But Shiner would not move. Then Ed would run ahead of him calling, "Come on, boy," and he'd pull us all over the ranch. Since Ed didn't have time to spend running all over the ranch ahead of Shiner, the whole idea pretty much failed. Shiner actually enjoyed climbing in the wagon while Warner or I pulled him around. When I was in the third grade, Warner and I found

Shiner dead out in front of the garage. He was thirteen and had just died of old age.

After Shiner, there were many dogs. I remember a cute little puppy I named Ginger. She was great company for me until she grew up and developed a very bad habit which led to her demise. She began sucking eggs. No matter what we did, she'd break into the chicken coup and take our eggs. I remember Mom and Elva, our foreman's wife, trying to console me as I sat on the kitchen step crying when she had to be shot.

Boots was Warner's dog, and I never forget the awful day when Warner had to rush to the house from the field to get the gun and shoot him after running over his legs with the hay mower. We both cried that day.

My favorite dog for many years was Margaret Lillian. Ed called her Midge. Her face looked like a well-used mop. She was always with me whether I was walking or riding a horse. I don't remember how she died, but I still have a lock of her hair in an envelope marked: *Margaret Lillian's Hair.*

I dressed my cats in doll dresses and pushed them around the ranch in a baby buggy. The cats would hunt for their food, but Ed poured fresh milk in a basin by the milk cellar for them every night. They would gather on the back porch and yowl whenever anybody stepped out the back door. The men, including my dad and Warner, would kick them into the ditch. Of course, I'd yell for them to stop, but before I could rescue them, they'd have already climbed out and shook themselves. The very next day, they'd be on the back porch screeching again.

The favorite place for cats to have kittens was in the barn. Ed would always come get me when he found a new litter. Some would grow up wild, so I'd tame them with food and sweet talk. I had a way with animals, so soon the cats felt comfortable enough to take up yowling on the back porch with the other cats. All my cats were named. I named one litter of kittens Tomia, Sophia, Delia, and Merhia. I pushed leppy lambs around in the baby buggy. We would have to bottle-feed them when a ewe died, and they'd follow me around the ranch after that.

I named an old hen, Maggie, when she became attached to me. She liked to roost on the foot of my cot outside at night, and she'd follow me around during the day. I'd even take her in the house with me. Maggie just wanted to be wherever I was. She was with me all one summer, but she died in the fall after we moved back to Ely. Everyone on the ranch thought Maggie was crazy or sick, but I didn't believe that. Research has been done on chickens, and they're found to be intelligent, and they seem to have souls. I think Maggie really loved me and was heartsick when I left her.

For a couple of years, Warner and I had a pet steer, Jimmy. The plan was that we'd feed and care for a steer, then auction him off in the fall, and keep the money for ourselves. It was to be a sort of 4-H project although neither of us knew what 4-H meant. Kathryn and Kent belonged to the 4-H in Alamo. What I remember is a little brown book called *I Dare You* that Kathryn got when she joined 4-H. I learned from that book that our lives should be divided into a square. One side stood for physical, one for mental, one social, and one spiritual. We should make sure we have developed all four parts of our square. I found a copy of *I Dare You* at a garage sale years later, so it is part of my library, and periodically I access my life by referring to that square.

After taking care of Jimmy for a year, both Warner and I had grown to love him. We brushed him and rode him around the corral almost every day. The night before the fair, Ed bathed him with Lux soap, rubbed him down, and curried him. He was very beautiful when Dad loaded him into the trailer for our trip to Ely. The next morning as Warner led Jimmy around the fair grounds, where people bid on him for prime beef, it hit Warner and me what was about to happen; and we both started crying and begging our dad not to sell Jimmy. I'm not sure whether someone bought Jimmy and my dad bought him back or whether Warner just took him out of the bidding area. I do know we brought Jimmy back home with us when the fair was over. The next fall when he was sold with the other steers, we accepted Jimmy's fate. Sometime during that year, Jimmy bloated from overfeeding, and Ed needed to "stick" him with a knife to release the gas. I remember wondering if we shouldn't have sold him according to the original plan.

In 1950, Dad sent away for a Norwegian elkhound from Billings, Montana. Monty was the only pedigree dog we ever had, and he caused us the most trouble. He was sick a lot, and he would not stay at home. He'd wonder to the next ranch and be gone for days. We took him to Ely with us during the week, but he'd dig under or jump over our fence there too. It is an understatement to say he brought out the worst in my father. Monty nearly ruined the only vacation I ever remember our family taking.

Daddy had decided our family would follow the trucks with our cattle to the feed lot in Imperial Valley, California, to make sure they got there safely. A vacation could be justified if it was also a business trip. We left the ranch and drove down the dirt road south to California where we had to stop at a check station. When the inspector opened our trunk, a gray eyeless creature jumped out. After it shook dust off for several seconds, we realized it was Monty. He had jumped in the trunk while we were packing. Miraculously he had not suffocated in the heat and dust. All we could do was load him in the backseat of our sedan with Warner, Bonnie, and me and continue our trip. We had to buy a rope, food, and a water dish; and we had to sneak him into the motels at night. It was hot, and Monty was dirty and smelly. The trip was not very enjoyable after that. Many months later, after searching for the source of a horrible smell in our car, Warner found a can of dog food which had been left in the trunk during our memorable "vacation."

It always broke my heart whenever one of my pets died or was killed, and I'd vow never to get attached to another one, but of course, I always did. The animals I had on the ranch were exactly what all of us want in a good friend. They were loyal, loving, accepting, and available when I needed them. I've continued to have pets throughout my lifetime, and I think I would say the animals in my life have been my best friends. When I get to Heaven, I expect to whistle and all the pets I've loved throughout my life including Shiner, Margaret Lillian, my mustang colt, Flicka, and even Maggie the hen will come running to me.

Sally with kittens in buggy

Warner with Shiner

Margaret Lillian

Sally on Bette

Sally on Jimmie the steer

12 Who Needs a Doctor?

There were only two times when we were growing up at Sunnyside that my parents had to take Warner or me to the doctor in Ely. Once I remember my mother and father taking turns yelling into the wall telephone above the desk in the dining room just outside my bedroom door. They were trying to explain to a doctor in Ely that I was having trouble breathing, and I seemed to be getting sicker by the minute. What could they do for me? All the usual treatments were not working. My parents were getting scared. Mom had rubbed my chest with Vicks VapoRub and placed towels heated on the oil stove in the living room over the rub. She had placed a vaporizer on the dining room table then lifted me up next to it and put a blanket over me. She had put me in a cool tub of water to lower my temperature. The doctor finally heard enough to demand that I be brought to Ely. My parents put blankets and a pillow on the backseat of our Mercury sedan, so I could sleep while we made the trip to town.

I had pneumonia and had to be kept in the hospital for several days where I was lonely and frightened even though either my mom or Aunt Jo were with me all the time. "We are running out of places to put shots in these skinny little arms," a nurse told my mother. I didn't really recover until I got back to the ranch.

The other trip they made to Ely was when Warner fell on a broken whiskey bottle in our creek and needed to have sixty stitches in his leg. That time a dish towel used as a tourniquet was added to Mom's arsenal of medical supplies. All the other times we were sick or hurt, my mother cared for us. When Warner or I fell off a haystack, out of a tree, or off a horse, we never broke any bones; so time healed our many bruises.

Mom got very good at treating burns while I was growing up. Once when Warner and I were very young, Mom put a hot apple pie in the wide window sill behind the kitchen sink. "Don't you kids get near my pie now," she told us as she went on to other tasks. We crept onto the counter and stared at the pie.

"Put your hand in it," Warner said to me. Without a thought, I did just what my four-year-old brother told me to do. Before Mom could get all the hot apples washed off my hand, I had second-degree burns. First she grabbed a tray of ice cubes and stuck my hand in ice water. Then she rubbed my hand with butter and wrapped it lightly with gauze.

"Stick your foot in there," was Warner's next suggestion that led to an even worse burn. Mom had warned us not to go near a kettle of hot grease she'd used to deep fry donuts in as she set it in the bedroom off the kitchen. That time I got third-degree burns on my foot. Mom again used ice cubes and then slathered my foot with Vaseline petroleum jelly and wrapped it with gauze and adhesive tape which she had to change several times a day because oozing liquid seeped through the gauze. My foot was one huge blister. I burned my foot again when Mom treated Warner and me for croup by putting us under a blanket on the dining room table with a vaporizer. I tipped the vaporizer over on my foot.

The worst burns I got was when I was running behind Daddy and Warner in a field of hot coals. My dad had burned all the trees he'd pulled out and dragged to an open lot next to the road. It had been weeks since the burn, so we didn't know there were still hot coals under the ashes. My boots were not as tall as my father's and brother's, so the coals got inside them. Before I could get them off, they blistered almost every part of both feet. By then Mom had learned to pour flour over my burns. Still I wore bedroom slippers for months before my feet healed enough so I could wear my boots again.

When I wasn't burning myself, my cousins were injuring me in one way or another. Orvis slammed my finger in the screen door; Mom put ice on it and kept it wrapped with gauze and tape until the nail came off. Kent ran me into barbed wire fence on my tricycle. I almost sliced off my little finger. I should have had stitches, but Mom used tape to keep the skin flat and it eventually healed.

Then my cousin Guy found an old bike in the dump (maybe one my father had owned when he was a boy) and restored it for me. He painted it Case tractor orange, and I couldn't wait to ride it. He assured my mother that he'd taught me how to ride. He just didn't tell her he hadn't taught me how to stop. I crashed into a big rock and skidded face-first into the gravel. That time Mom stretched me out on the long dining room table, and she and Guy picked rocks out of the skin on my face, elbows, and knees, then they poured a whole bottle of iodine all over me.

Almost any accident could be treated with the very select medicines in my mother's medicine shelf above the spices. Vick's VapoRub, Vaseline, Mentholatum, Absorbine Jr., rubbing alcohol, castor oil, iodine, merthiolate, Band-Aids, gauze, adhesive tape, and aspirin. Any bottles with any alcohol content, including rubbing alcohol and vanilla extract, were moved to a drawer in the desk and locked up when my parents left the ranch because the hired men would sneak into the house and drink them.

I keep every one of those first-aid supplies in my own home, and they served me well when I was raising my own children. I recall all the doctors I've been to since I left the ranch, and I wonder how many times I really needed to see them. I'm not saying my mother could have cured all my ailments with her medical skills and small shelf of medicines, but her treatments worked when I was young, and none of them caused any side effects.

Sally on bike Guy fixed for me

13 The Telephone

When my dad picked up the receiver on our dining room wall phone and found it dead, he threw it back at the wall and shouted, "What would be the matter with those fools stringing the wire back on the pole when they knock the line down?"

The telephone poles marched across the alkali flat like tired soldiers carrying news home from WWII. The phone lines strung on the tall power poles connected the ranches in White River Valley to Lund and then to Ely. Lightning, wind, or even a cow scratching on a pole could knock the line down, and it was usually up to my father to saddle his horse and follow the telephone line for several miles until he found the problem.

Daddy was trying to get a call through to Tonopah, the county seat of Nye County, concerning the condition of the thirty-five miles of gravel road between Lund and Sunnyside. The road was no longer gravel at all. Storms and the road grader, itself, had washed or scraped all the gravel over to the shoulder. What was left on the road was hard top and boulders. The road had become almost impossible to negotiate. He wanted Nye County to send a grader over right away because it had recently rained, and it was a good time to do the roadwork. The road also needed to be regraveled, but that never happened.

Sunnyside was located near the corner of three counties: White Pine, Lincoln, and Nye. Unfortunately, it was situated closest to White Pine and Lincoln counties but was actually in Nye County, the largest county in Nevada. That caused a problem. It took a road grader most of a day to go the 210 miles from Tonopah to Sunnyside. We were lucky if it came twice a year. Usually they sent a grader over after a long dry spell when the blade did more damage than good.

The Hendrixes, who lived on the ranch three miles south of Sunnyside, drove to Lund a couple of times a week even though the roads were terrible and caused wear and tear on their cars. My dad found it unbelievable that Alice Hendrix would drive her daughter, Marilyn, to dance lessons once a week in Lund. Did she realize the time she wasted when she could be doing work that needed to be done on the ranch? I wished my dad would have allowed Bonnie to go to dance lessons too. She might have been happier to stay on the ranch during the summers.

The Riordans lived on the ranch twelve miles north of our ranch. Lawrence made many more trips to Ely than we did. The bars in Ely could be compared to CNN or Fox News, and we were lucky to have Lawrence relating important news to us by phone when he made it back to the ranch after his visits to those bars. (His wife didn't see his trips to the bars as lucky for her, and she eventually divorced him and left the ranch.) Since nobody left our ranch unless we needed a part for the machinery or for the occasional trip to town for staples, the telephone was important to us.

There were usually only three reasons for us to get a phone call: emergencies, news of world-changing events, and word that someone was on the way to visit us. Did we need anything? It was exciting for me when I heard the telephone ring—especially when there were three longs and two short rings made by someone turning the crank on the side of a telephone somewhere down the line. That was our ring.

One afternoon, the phone rang one long steady ring. That always meant an emergency. Fortunately my dad and several hired men were nearby when Mom related the message that there was a fire at Hendrixes'. Everyone grabbed a bucket, shovel, or hose and headed over there to find an old bunkhouse on fire. Two Hendrix children had been playing with matches. By the time people from the Riordan Ranch, twelve miles away, and from Lund got there, we had formed a bucket brigade from the creek, and the fire was almost under control. We had saved the haystack and the livestock which was probably more important than saving the ranch house and the wife.

My mother told of twice lying awake in the night, waiting for the phone to ring. Both times she had a strong "feeling" that something was wrong with her family. Both times she did get a call. Grandma called to say she'd had to drive Grandpa to the hospital in Ely from their Baker Ranch. The other time Grandpa called to say Mabel had attempted suicide, and he had to take a train across country to New York so she could be released from a mental hospital and brought back to Nevada.

I was only six years old, but I remember when Lawrence Riordan called my mother to tell her that President Roosevelt had died and later to tell her that World War II was over. I didn't know anything about President

Roosevelt, but I was happy about the war being over because Mom told me we would no longer need ration books for sugar or gasoline. Now she could make more trips to town and buy more Log Cabin syrup so Warner and I could have the cans for buildings on our farm.

Dale Carter, who owned the small store in Lund with her husband, Arthur, was the telephone operator and could be reached by cranking one long, long ring on the phone. Sometimes she was able to get a call through to Ely like the time when I was eight years old and had pneumonia.

One windy afternoon, Mom answered a call from the cattle buyer who had recently negotiated a great deal with my father. He was backing out. Ranchers only get one paycheck a year when they sell their cows in the fall. This deal would have seen us through the year very nicely. When my mother told Daddy the bad news, he was furious with her. She had obviously said something on the phone to anger the cattle buyer, he told her. This was all her fault. I understand the frustration he must have felt, and I'm sure Mom did too because she did not try to defend herself. I was angry with her at the time because I thought she was weak and should not have allowed herself to be treated that way. Now I look back, and I can imagine how disappointed Daddy must have been. My mother understood his disappointment and allowed him to vent on her. I don't know if that is a strength or a weakness, but that was who my mother was.

14 Baby Sister

They were here! When my dad began honking the horn, I tipped the bench I was sitting on backward, scattering piano books all over the living room. I couldn't believe that I would finally be seeing my baby sister and that my mother would be coming back home. It had been too cold to stay up at the road to watch for a dust from the car, so I kept coming back to the house to practice the piano. Now, finally, they were driving into the yard.

Mom had been living in town, sixty-five miles away with Aunt Jo, for weeks waiting to go into labor. Things had gotten so desperate here on the ranch without Mom that Daddy had hired a cook. Old Lady Leland. We'd never seen her before, and she was kind of mean to Warner and me. My most vivid memory was the soup incident. She told Warner to ring the dinner bell as she lifted the soup pot from the stove. When she stepped up from the kitchen to the dining room, she tripped and soup poured all over the dining room floor. She began yelling for Warner and me to get spoons and scoop as much soup back into the pan as we could while she grabbed the mop and cleaned up what was left. Miraculously, there was still some soup in the pot, and it was setting on the table when the hired men began to sit down. I don't think they suspected anything, but I also don't think it would have mattered. They had no choice but to eat the food because there were no stores or restaurants anywhere nearby. Later when Warner and I told Mom about the incident, she was not amused. Old Lady Leland was long gone by then, however.

Now Mother was back home; all of our troubles would be over. My father came around the car to help Mom out with this new baby, Bonnie Claire. She was beautiful, and my father was obviously smitten with her. It took me about thirty minutes to figure out that my life was never going to be the same again. And the change was not going to be for the better.

What had gone wrong? I would be an old lady before this baby would ever be the playmate I longed for. She wouldn't be able to play games or dolls with me for years, and she took up what little time my mother had had for me. She needed to be fed and changed constantly, and she cried half the night. The floor squeaked night after night outside my bedroom door as my father walked back and forth holding Bonnie and singing to her.

"Don't cry my little buckaroo
The great oak tree was once an acorn like you"

I had my eighth birthday three weeks after Bonnie arrived at the ranch, but there was barely an acknowledgment. She seemed to take all the available time and energy, and she got all the attention. My new baby sister was so cute and smart that Ed Rowlie would find reasons to hang around the house so he could hold her, play with her, and laugh at her. Aunt Jo, who always thought the sun rose and set in Warner and me, now doted on Bonnie when she came to visit at the ranch. Bonnie was walking and putting words together in sentences at nine months. She was definitely a special child, but I was disliking her more every day.

Then one afternoon when she about two years old, Bonnie disappeared. Mom and Aunt Ruth were busy with things that always needed to be done when Aunt Ruth said, "Where is Bonnie Claire?"

Time stopped, and everybody on the ranch began searching in different directions. The first place we looked was in the creek behind the house. I had almost drowned there when I had escaped out the back door at about sixteen months old and had fallen in the creek. I was already being sucked head first under the cement bridge when my mother found me. Mother was sure that was what had happened to Bonnie. We poked under the bridge with a stick and nothing came out the other side, so we began running downstream, thinking she had fallen in somewhere below the bridge. I could picture her floating facedown in the ditch. Someone ran up to the highway. Fortunately, a car had not gone by all day, so she would not have been run over. We called her name as we searched in every direction. She was nowhere to be found, and we were frantic. It was now getting late afternoon.

I was crying as I ran through the house thinking I would go up to the head of the spring and then follow the creek all the way down to the reservoir when I heard a faint sound coming from the bedroom off the kitchen. I opened the door and found Bonnie crouched between the bed and the dressing table. She had every bit of makeup out of Aunt Ruth's overnight case and was busy painting her face, arms, and legs as well as the floor and walls. I think she knew we were searching for her, but she was having far too much fun for a toddler to resist.

So I was the hero; I had found Bonnie. That night as I watched her sleeping in her crib, I realized what a beautiful child she was and how much I loved her, and I realized how upset I would have been if something had happened to her.

Bonnie never was company for me on the ranch. In fact, instead of playing dolls with me, she pulled my dolls' hair out and lost their clothes. All the dolls that I had carefully saved since I was three or four years old were being ruined. I had to share a bedroom with Bonnie, and there was no safe place for my things.

My last doll was a beautiful Toni doll with platinum blonde hair which I got for Christmas in 1950. I named her Candy. She came with a cardboard wardrobe to hold a real mink cape my grandmother had made from her muff, a silk evening gown, a night gown, and a cotton dress that Grandma also made. I was never real comfortable with my mother's mother. She seemed cold, judgmental, and critical of me, but she was very ambitious and creative, and I appreciated the time she spent on Candy's clothes. She once made me a wooden cupboard with glass doors that I used in my playhouse at the ranch to put my dishes in.

Toni dolls were the first dolls ever made with hair that could be combed and styled. They were named after the Toni home permanents. Perm curlers and a solution for giving permanents came with them. When I ran out of that solutions, I used sugar and water which worked just as well. Bonnie got a smaller Toni doll with black hair, but she decided she did not like her doll and wanted to play with Candy. When I complained to my mother, she told me, "It won't hurt for you to let Bonnie play with your doll." That was it! I'd had enough of my baby sister. I threw the biggest tantrum of my life. Fortunately, Mother's friend, Reva Brown, who was visiting, pointed out what my mother was too busy to see. I had nothing of my own and was being forced to give up everything for Bonnie. Once my mother realized what was happening, she told me I could keep everything I cared about on top of the wardrobe in the bedroom I shared with Bonnie. She was never allowed to touch Candy again. Even though she was still determined to play with her, Candy survived, and today she has a special place on a shelf in my home.

Unlike Warner and me, Bonnie hated the ranch. She never bought into the idea that the ranch belonged to the family, and we all needed to work together to make it successful. My mother spoiled her because she felt guilty for making Bonnie come to the ranch, so she accommodated her every demand. She'd sometimes fix three breakfasts before Bonnie would eat. She never said no or set any boundaries that I could see. Maybe she was just worn out and gave up on parenting entirely. Once I asked my mother, "Mom, why didn't you ask me if I wanted a baby before you had Bonnie?" I really felt I was raising her.

My dad tried, but he was dealing with an entirely different personality than Warner or me. If he had let her go to dance classes like Marilyn Hendrix on the next ranch or had done anything to make her happier, things might have been better. He always felt Bonnie should be exactly like me. The two of them clashed from the day she learned the word "no." By the time I graduated from high school, I could see that Bonnie was way out of control. I had never cared much about boys at all, but at ten years old she was "dating." I confronted my parents about that. They didn't seem to have a clue what to do with Bonnie.

For Bonnie's part, she once told me the only thing she remembers from her childhood is that she was always in someone's way.

"I can't answer for anyone else," I told her, "but you sure were always in my way."

When Bonnie was thirteen and I was twenty-one, married, with a baby, and living in Alaska, I got the phone call from my dad. "I can't do this anymore," he told me. "I need to send Bonnie to live with you." They drove her the 2500 miles up the Alcan Highway. I thought Daddy looked like he'd aged ten years when they arrived at the door of our army housing quarters on the base late one night. He once told me the hardest thing he ever did in his life was to raise Bonnie.

Not long ago, Bonnie told me about the time she tried to file a child abuse charge against my dad. They were having a huge fight, and Daddy knocked her backward into a recliner so hard the back legs broke off. She hit her head on the windowsill. Armed with a knot on the back of her head for evidence, she marched off to the sheriff's office. The sheriff was my mother's cousin. "Bonnie, you are a spoiled little brat; you straighten up and get yourself home, or I'll knock you around," he told her. I was amazed to hear her story. Never would I have had the nerve to do such a thing. I did ask her why he'd gotten so angry at her.

"I never said I was perfect," she answered. "I had sneaked out with a kid old enough to drive when I was still in grade school."

Bonnie lived with us for one summer and half a school year. She didn't cause me any trouble and to my surprise, I enjoyed having her with me as I was very homesick. She flew home for Christmas and decided she wanted to finish high school in Ely. I packed her clothes and mailed them back to her. Things were better for them, but she got married at age seventeen. Daddy was pleased. "I would never have guessed Bonnie would marry such a good man," he said to me. Doug was going to college and then was going on to law school. Doug and Bonnie are still married.

Many decades later, my little sister has become a smart businesswoman owning her own cruise business. She is a wife and mother and is finally the friend I needed so badly on the ranch in the 1940s.

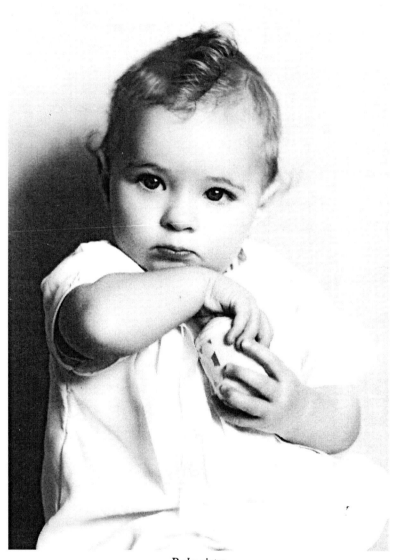

Baby sister

Sally with Bonnie Claire

Bonnie age 16

15 Forever Churning

The most time-consuming job of my young life was churning the cream into butter. I always made sure I had a couple of funny books to read as I turned the handle. *Little Lulu* and *Sniffles* were my two favorites. There was very little else to read, so I'd read them over and over. Sniffles was a little mouse whose best friend was Mary Jane, a girl about my age, seven or eight. She could throw magic dust in the air and say, "Poof, poof piffles; make me small like Sniffles." Immediately she'd become mouse-sized, and the two friends were off on all kinds of adventures. They'd ride pieces of bark down the river or climb under leaves or crawl into containers and holes. Usually they'd get themselves into trouble.

I read while I churned for sometimes an hour or more—depending on how much cream Ed had separated. Daddy only liked butter made from sweet cream, so that always took longer to churn. Each morning Ed would rinse the cream separator in the creek and bring the huge stainless steel bowl and all the individual parts into the kitchen for my mother and me to wash and scald. Then he'd put a jar of cream into the fridge. It took at least three gallons to fill the churn. Mom made three loaves of bread every other day, so I liked to coordinate my churning day with her bread day. She'd stand elbow deep in flour, kneading a huge batch of dough while I churned. I felt happy and safe working next to my mother.

"Don't waste time lifting the lid," Mom told me. "Just keep churning until it begins to gather." Eventually the steady splashing sound changed to a sloshing, and the feel of the crank changed. The cream had turned to butter. I'd churn for about five more minutes to make sure the butter and buttermilk had separated (gathered). Mom would then help me lift the round wooden churn up to the sink where we'd pull the plug at the bottom and drain the buttermilk into a jar for Ed to have for lunch or for Mom to cook with. Then we'd pull out the butter paddles and scrape the butter into a wooden bowl so I could begin "working" it by using a flat wooden spatula to squeeze out the buttermilk. As I worked, I'd run icy cold water from the faucet over it and drain off the liquid until only the butter was left in the bowl. Sometimes that process would take thirty minutes. Then I'd add a little salt, work it some more, and put the butter into the butter mold. After I pressed it into a pound, I'd wrap it in waxed paper and put it in the fridge.

When I was first learning the process, my mother noticed that the butter was not separating from the buttermilk. She couldn't figure out the problem until she noticed I was using water from the hot water tap to work my butter. When she mentioned it to Ed, it became the topic of conversation for several meals, and all the men got a good laugh.

One morning, Daddy came into the kitchen, sat down with a leftover cup of coffee, and came up with an idea to shorten my churning time. He would hook up a motor to the churn handle. The problem was the only motor he had was too big for the churn. "You'll need to sit on the lid." Daddy told me. "Just read your comic books while the motor does the work." I don't think he explained the importance of that simple task.

So life was good. The churn sat on the kitchen table, and I sat on the churn happily reading. Then one morning, probably as Mary Jane and Sniffles were involved in an exciting adventure, I forgot about my job, and I stood up. My dad stepped through the kitchen door just as the churn lid hit the ceiling where it was held by a geyser of butter chunks and buttermilk. Typical of his explosive personality, he grabbed the churn and with the motor still running pitched them both out the back door into the creek. Nobody needed to tell Ed the exciting news because we were still cleaning up the mess when the men came into the kitchen for lunch.

As I helped my parents scrub butter and buttermilk from the ceiling, walls, tables, cupboards, window, and floor, I knew we would be getting a new churn, and I was also sure I'd be cranking it by hand for the rest of my natural life. Because of me, Daddy's sweet thoughtful idea to make my life easier had turned very, very sour.

16 *Making Jerky*

Nothing "curdled my mother's blood," according to her, like Daddy's announcement that "Tomorrow seems like a pretty good day to make jerky." Mother had known the time was getting close. Dad had been sitting at the kitchen table, sharpening butcher knives for several evenings. He had been checking his jerky lines strung on the fence below the house to make sure none of them had broken during the winter, and there did not seem to be any signs of a storm coming. Also the halves of beef had been aging for at least a week. They were hung outside when the evenings got cool and then were brought back into the basement every morning when the sun and the flies came out. Without refrigeration, this chore was necessary, so the meat would not spoil. Still, before we got a walk-in freezer, I remember quarters of beef being carried to the pigs because we didn't eat it fast enough.

None of this steer would be wasted, though, not when it was used for jerky. Daddy saved out steaks and other prime cuts before he began slicing the meat into small approximately two-by-four-inch strips—cross grain. "You always cut meat for jerky cross grain," he told Warner and me when we got old enough to handle Dad's razor-sharp butcher knives. "You'll never get a piece of meat to hang on a line if you don't." Until we were old enough to help with the cutting, my dad planned his jerky-making day to coincide with the Boss's (Grandpa Whipple's) visit.

Mother told a story of one very, very windy jerky-making day when the wind was howling through the fifty-year-old cottonwood trees, and no other sounds on the ranch could be heard. That morning, she needed to make a trip to the basement where all of our food supply was stored. When she left, she automatically slipped the hook into the latch on the outside of the basement door, as she always did, and went on back to the house to begin cooking for the day. Hours later, she rang the bell for lunch. When Grandpa and Daddy did not come to eat, she went to investigate. She found the two men yelling at the top of their lungs to be let out of the basement, and they were not happy men. Quickly she unlatched the hook and ran up the basement stairs as fast as she could to the house. By their own rules, swearing was not allowed in front of women (or at women) on the ranch. It was a good thing because "the air would have been blue" that day, my mother told me.

In the early afternoon, Dad began bringing in the big pots to set on the propane burners. He filled them with warm water, placed one raw egg in each pot, and dumped salt into the water until the raw eggs came to the top indicating that enough salt had been added. Next we all began carrying large dishpans full of cut meat to the kitchen. The mess was about to begin.

We each took a pot and dropped in the pieces of meat just until they turned white—one minute at the most. Large spoons with holes were used to move the meat back to the pans where we peppered it, one layer at a time. We used cans of black pepper because no fly or bug or animal would bother the meat while it hung on the outside lines with all that pepper on it. The jerky never seemed too spicy, so the pepper taste must have weakened in the drying process.

Finally we carried the pans outside where we hung the small slabs of meat, one piece at a time, over the lines. Because the meat had been carefully sliced cross grain, each piece hung tightly in place. With four or five of us working, this job still took several hours. We were lucky to be finished by supper time. We were also lucky if the weather held, and there were no storms for the three to five days it took for the meat to dry. A few times we all needed to rush back out with pans when it began to rain and bring in all the meat. It was never as easy to get it to hang on the lines the second time we put it out. Once we did this whole hanging process three times before the meat was dried.

Mother then began cleaning the kitchen. Salt, salty water, blood, bloody water, tiny pieces of meat, and pepper covered the stove as well as most of the kitchen. She had to get the kitchen clean enough that night so she could cook supper. Then she spent the next day really scrubbing and cleaning up the mess.

Making jerky was one of the most important jobs on the ranch. We made venison jerky in the fall and beef jerky in the spring. It was a staple of our food storage just like sugar, flour, and salt. Nobody ever left the ranch on horse or in the truck or car without a sack of jerky and a canteen of water. Hour after hour, my dad would ride along on horseback, eating pieces of jerky. He ate it by slicing off tiny slivers of dried meat with his always razor-sharp pocketknife and then eating them from the blade. This would be all he would eat from breakfast until he got home sometimes at ten or eleven o'clock at night. Making jerky was a hard and dirty job, but it was as important to the ranchers as putting up hay was to their livestock.

Aunt Ruth watching jerky dry

17 *Fifty Years of Cattle Ranching in Eastern Nevada*

When my grandfather bought Sunnyside Ranch in 1904, the ranchers ran their cattle on government land "in common." That meant there were no fences, boundaries, or allotments. Cattle from the ranches in White River Valley grazed on the 250,000 acres freely with no controls.

By the time my father bought the ranch in 1936, the land had been allocated by the Taylor Grazing Act of 1934 which established how many and where the cattle and sheep could run. It was managed by the Bureau of Land Management (BLM) under the Department of the Interior. The number of livestock allotted to each ranch was determined by a unit of measurement called an AUM or animal units per month. An AUM was one cow with a calf that was under nine months of age. For sheep it was five sheep equaled one AUM and two AUMs equaled one horse. Ranchers were charged grazing fees. The largest problem with open-range grazing was, and still is, that cattle and sheep can't share the same land. Sheep mow the plant down to the root, leaving nothing for the cows to graze on. Cattle eat by rolling their tongue around the stalk of the plant and sucking the nutrients, leaving the plant intact to grow back fairly quickly.

A few guys from Alamo were with Kathryn and me one night, and they determined that I would be the more valuable date because my dad had more AUMs. None of them asked me for a date, however. It was "cowboy humor."

Between 1940 and 1945, the ranchers and the government spent years meeting to determine the allotments. Ranchers were asked to check their guns at the door as many of those meetings got very heated. The land was being overgrazed, so the ranchers were allotted less land and charged higher fees. Mustangs became a serious problem for the ranchers. Wild horses have no natural enemy, so there were thousands grazing on what good feed was available. More seriously, herds of them would take over the few water holes on the range, not letting cattle have water. One mustang can drink twenty or thirty gallons of water a day. "Mustanging" became a solution. They were herded into makeshift corrals and trucked out to glue factories.

By then, the BLM began to survey public land and to establish carrying capacity and set the number of livestock to be grazed. I once heard that a BLM employee measured a rancher's haystack to determine how many cattle he could feed and how much public land he should have. Since most ranchers owned more cattle than their own land would support, they depended upon public land. Following those surveys, everyone's herds had to be reduced. In our home, there was nothing more hated than the &$%# BLM.

By the late 1950s and early 1960s, it became apparent to the BLM that range conditions were still deteriorating. Further livestock reductions were required, and those requirements were placed into effect by legal decisions. All this was taking place before taking into account the wild horses, deer, antelope, and other wild animals as well as steep ground where animals could not graze and the many acres where water was not available. After the allotments were defined, the ranchers in the White River Valley ran their cattle within those established boundaries while the sheep grazed around the outskirts of the range in the higher mountains. Basque sheep herders lived isolated lives in tents or sheep wagons while making sure the sheep grazed only on their allotted land and coyotes and bobcats did not get the lambs. One particular sheep man had no problem letting his sheep run on my father's allotted land. More than once Daddy threatened to kill him.

Since boundary lines were determined by mountain ranges, streams, and other natural features of the land, the cattle crossed boundaries, and all ended up grazing together. Even cattle from the ranches one hundred miles south in Pahranagat Valley would drift from Coal Valley into the sink of White River during the winter. Springs and wells, improved and built by the boys stationed at the CCC (Civilian Conservation Corps) camp near Sunnyside in the 1930s and 1940s, were scattered within those boundaries.

When a winter was wet and the range was green, the cattle did not need to wander too far away from water to find feed. That made it a little easier for cowboys to gather the cattle in the early spring for separating and branding. These cattle were wild and did not take to being herded very well. At best it would take two weeks of riding to find the majority of the cattle that had been wintering in the sink of White River Valley. On dry years it took several weeks to gather cattle.

The ranchers shut down the wells before the branding, so the cattle were forced to drift toward the only other water which was Murphy Meadows. All the cattle were herded to the fenced fields at Murphy Meadows. Once there, it took several more days for the ranchers to separate their cattle so the calves could be branded. Pahranagat Valley ranchers: Wrights, Higbys, Murray Whipple, Stewarts, and Wadsworths rode the 250,000 acres with White River ranchers: Riordans (later Adams), Clair Whipple, and Hendrixes.

The calves had to be "mothered up" before they could be branded. The mother's brand determined whose brand to put on the calf. When all the calves were branded, the men had long cattle drives ahead of them. The cowboys from ranches in Pahranagat Valley drove their cattle south to summer in Coal Valley. The Murray Whipple and Riordan's ranches summered their cattle north with ours. Ten to twenty cowboys drove as many as eight thousand head of cattle to the summer range in Cave Valley in three separate drives.

The first drive was with the "dry" cows and the cows that had not calved yet. They stopped two nights on that drive—once at Blind Springs and then at Long Water. Two more days were spent pushing the cattle higher into the mountains where they would summer at Sheep Camp, Willow Creek, and Cattle Camp. The fourth night they unsaddled their horses, turned them loose, and drove back to Sunnyside in the truck.

The cowboys were up at "the crack of dawn" the next morning. After breakfast they fed their horses which had made it back to the ranch during the night. Then they headed back to Murphy Meadows to make the slower and harder sixty-mile drive to the summer range with the cows and newly branded calves.

Next they rode back to all the water holes in the sink of White River locating all the cattle they had missed on the first two drives. That time they went up the other side of the valley starting at the lower end of Cave Valley from Big Springs to Lewis Well and Silver King. They held the cows at the Windmill and branded all the calves they'd found along the way. They turned them all loose at the Big Springs wash the fifth day as the cattle were far enough into Cave Valley to stay the summer.

Here I am going to quote an excerpt from a story written by Dave Mathis, a friend of my cousin, Guy, who took part in this "bona fide open range cattle drive" during a summer vacation. He was sixteen at the time, but he never forgot the experience.

Punk had given me an ugly bally faced bay named Rambler.
Most of the other saddle horses were half or better thoroughbred.
If Rambler had any hot blood it was buried well below the

surface. I'd been riding horses since I was four and Rambler dinged my ego. I saddled him with reluctance. Punk's thinking, though, was solid. He had no question about what that horse knew or could do.

Punk, nine-year-old Warner, and myself rode to the south end of Cave Valley leading a cavvy of horses from the home ranch of Sunnyside to Lewis Well, twenty miles away. There we met the chuck wagon and other friends and relatives who were going to help. After dinner we unloaded cowboy bedrolls, saddles, hay, and grain out of the truck. We slept on the ground and as the song goes, "The stars were our ceiling."

The sun hadn't made an effort to get up when we rolled out the next morning. We grained the horses using gunny sack nosebags. George the cook yelled, and we went to breakfast. There were eggs, sourdough biscuits, and gravy made from side pork and can milk. The strong cowboy coffee was boiling. Almost as soon as the sun lit the area we began seeing cattle (all Herefords in those days), but we rode by them. When we got to where Punk knew was the southern limit of his cattle drift, we went to work. A couple of riders went to Silver King to gather what might be there. The rest of us began moving up the lower end of Cave Valley, about four and five miles wide. Cows then in that country were wild, only being handled twice a year—once in the spring and again in the fall. When we were still two hundred to three hundred yards away they spooked, throwing up their heads, hiking their tails, blowing, and taking off on the run. We were fanned out, though, so kept the cattle ahead and running up the valley. Then out of the blue I heard a war whoop and saw Punk push his good-looking sorrel, Diamond, into a full gallop. Everybody followed suit. What a show. Cattle and cowboys charging full speed up the valley. It was wild with dust aplenty. Ugly old Rambler was skimming along, staying with the classy horses, clearing sagebrush and washes. I became aware that a couple of things were happening. We were picking up small groups of cattle as we went, bunching up, fusing increasingly into a herd.

All of a sudden, Punk shifted the sorrel into overdrive. Now on a dead run, he passed me and sidled up closer to the stampeding cows. Soon he was even with the leaders. He turned them back into the herd, causing the animals to circle. Guy, Alan, Warner, and I helped stop the bunch. Now all riders moved out to a position to hold the animals and let them settle down. I figured the wild ride served a number of purposes. First, the cows were going to run anyway; second, it took a lot of wild out of cows short on energy because of sparse winter feed . . . and dam, it was fun. The stopping allowed the calves to mother up, the herd to settle, and the Silver King riders to catch up.

After that cattle drive was over, my father and several cowboys camped at the Hagerty Ranch in Cave Valley. They spent a week pushing all the cattle even higher into the mountains. Having taken a month to get all the cattle to the summer range, it was now the first week of July. The cowboys returned to the ranch, hung up their saddles and bridles, started up the tractors, and began "haying." A few of the true buckaroos Dad had hired moved on for they would have nothing to do with machinery.

A successful year of haying, the second most important job for cattle ranchers, depended entirely on the weather. If it rained enough for the alfalfa to grow and be mowed, raked, and baled three times, it was a good year. Two crops were the norm. If it rained too much, the fields were flooded. Flash floods could take out entire fields, and Daddy would need to replant the alfalfa seed and start over. By September, all the bales of alfalfa and meadow hay for the year had been stacked and were now ready for winter feeding.

With the hay put up, it was time to go riding again to bring all the cattle back out of the mountains. Many had already started drifting down. Some were driven, and some were trucked to Sunnyside. One of the sounds of fall on the ranch was the cows and calves bawling all day and night for a week or so after the calves were weaned from their mothers. The calves were then fed alfalfa for a month or two to fatten them up before they were ready for the sale.

The cows not being sold were pushed back to the sink of White River Valley. There they would, hopefully, winter well enough to have a healthy calf crop in the spring. Daddy hired a man (usually Basque) to live down at the sink all winter and watch over the cattle. His job was to ride on horseback to all the wells and water holes, making sure the pumps were running and the mustangs weren't keeping the cattle away from the water holes. Once a month, Daddy would haul supplies to him. Beans were the staple.

It was exciting for me every fall when the huge cattle trucks pulled into the yard above the ranch in the night. I asked to see inside them and decided I'd be very happy driving cattle trucks. We could count on my dad being in high spirits when those trucks loaded with our cattle drove out of our yard. He had just gotten his one and only paycheck for the year. In a good year, the cattle came out of the mountains fat, and my dad got a fair price for the calves. Daddy and Mom made a trip to the bank in Ely where the check was deposited; they were able to pay their bills and have plenty to live on for the year.

My dad spent his winters oiling and conditioning his saddle and bridles in the dining room. He'd also scrape hair and flesh from cowhide and cut it in strips which he'd braid into ropes and horse gear. He made several reatas (catch ropes) by braiding rawhide. I remember Daddy made a rope out of hemp and nylon (a material invented during WWII). He started it by tying it to the bedroom doorknob.

My dad bought a Cessna 172 airplane which we were able to spot cattle with and fly back and forth to Ely in. When we moved to town in the fall of 1948, my parents could afford to pay cash for a house and all the furnishings and still have $70,000 in the bank with no debt. Those were good years; we were "well fixed."

Lila and Punk at Sunnyside next to Cessna 172

Steers ready for sale in fall

Warner 'haying'

Clair working cattle at the ranch

'Home on the range' for Clair

18 Branding at Murphy Meadows

Mom's potato cake iced with her cooked icing and sprinkled with nuts was not just a dessert; it was an event. It was Daddy's favorite, and every year the branding at Murphy Meadows fell on June 6, his birthday. Mom brought the cake to Murphy Meadows in a very large sheet cake pan. She carried a huge pot of chili beans or a mulligan stew (a beef stew with macaroni) in a cow camp kettle which had clamps to hold its lid on. She also brought pans of homemade hot rolls and fresh vegetables from the garden—lettuce, tomatoes, radishes, and onions. Cowboys from Pahranagat Valley and White River Valley always gathered for the branding and for my father's birthday. Usually one or two of my aunts would help Mom, but later just she and I would cook and deliver the meal, then haul the dirty pots and dishes back to Sunnyside. Many times there would be as many as thirty cowboys from at least eight outfits involved in the branding.

There was a large corral and a meadow at Murphy Meadows—but no trees. My dad built a canvas shelter stretched over posts where we put a table for the food. Everyone sat in the powder-soft alkali dirt—except for my father who was honored by getting to sit on a folding chair. We'd balance our tin plates on our laps and drink fresh lemonade or strong hot coffee. I'd find a little shade from the truck or sheep wagon. Usually the wind was blowing dirt in our eyes, mouth, and food. My lips felt gritty and tasted bitter when I ran my tongue along them.

Everybody was happy as they mulled around the camp, eating Mom's wonderful food and discussing the branding that had been going on for several hours before we arrived with the dinner. Then Mom and I brought out Daddy's birthday cake, and we all sang to him. The wind usually blew out the candles before he got the chance to. We served the cake with dust blowing in our faces. The cowboys took a large piece in their hands which had been rubbed clean in the dirt and wiped on their pant legs.

The branders rested only a few minutes before they added brush to the branding fire and went back to work. Daddy was always the roper. Before Uncle Murray died, he and Murray took turns lassoing the hind legs of the calves. Both were able to make a perfect catch every time. Even though lassoing the hind legs is harder than the head, they didn't like the idea of dragging a calf by the neck.

The strong smell of burning hide filled the air as the iron burned the ranchers' brands into the calf's flank or side. Daddy's brand was a cross on both flanks; mine was a cross on the side, and Warner's was a VA on the right flank. The Murray Whipple brand was a seventy on the right flank. Each rancher had his own registered brand. The calf would be earmarked with the whack of a knife and the male calves castrated. It was hot, exhausting work which required team effort. Every man knew his job, from roping the calf, to keeping a hot fire going, to running the branding irons, to positioning the calf, to holding the herd.

The day after the branding, the cowboys rolled up their bedrolls and broke camp. They had many long days of cattle driving ahead of them. The ranchers from Pahranagat Valley drove their cattle south to Coal Valley. Since The Murray Whipple Ranch summered their cattle in Cave Valley, they drove their herd along with ours fifty miles north to the summer range.

Breaking for lunch at Murphy Meadows

Daddy celebrates birthday while branding at Murphy Meadows

19 Six-Year-Old Cowhand

The year after Uncle Murray died, my father allowed me to take part in the largest cattle drive from Murphy Meadows to the summer range in the mountains of Cave Valley. We would be pushing a thousand head of cows and newly branded calves. Early the morning after the branding at Murphy Meadows, Dad made a breakfast of sourdough pancakes, eggs and bacon, and strong coffee served in tin cups. Everyone rolled up their bedrolls and packed up the truck. Daddy rolled the quarter of beef he'd hung outside the night before into a bedroll to keep it cool inside the sheep wagon during the day. Then he loaded everything else up and prepared to pull the sheep wagon to where we would camp the first night.

My horse Fidget was old. He had been Guy's horse, then Warner's horse. He had not forgotten his training as a cow horse though. As I straddled him hour after hour, I knew that I could nod off, and he would still bring a stray cow or calf back to the herd. Fidget and I rode the drag, following behind the herd of cattle and riding back and forth "pushing" the calves and older, slower cows. Occasionally a calf would get too tired to go any farther, and one of the cowboys would lay it across the front of my saddle. I loved the company. My brother's old hand-me-down hat shaded my eyes, and my white leather chaps kept the skin from rubbing off my legs. Like all the other cow hands, I had a canteen of water and sack of jerky. I was a happy little white-haired cowgal.

We made it to the dam, which was our first stop, in the late afternoon of the first day. All the calves had fallen behind, so the cowboys had several more hours "mothering" them up. The calves were hungry, and only their mothers would allow them to feed. As the cowboys held the herd, the cows would head to the rear where their calves were bawling. Kent seemed to have a knack for matching calves to their mothers better than anyone else, even though he was only six years old. He was a natural-born cowboy just like his father—my Uncle Murray.

Once we stopped herding, though, my day was over. I slid off Fidget and walked slowly toward the sheep wagon. It took a few seconds for my legs to adjust to walking after sitting on the horse for so many hours. My father poured me hot water from the teakettle into a wash basin on the step of the sheep wagon. Then he handed me a bar of Lifebuoy soap, and I began lathering my grimy hands and rinsing my hands and face in the warm water. I dried with a small unclean towel lying nearby. Streaks of dirt ran down each side of my face, and my teeth were gritty with dust and dried manure that had blown in my face all day. Soon Daddy had fried potatoes and onions and meat with pork and beans ready to serve the cowboys as they took turns coming for food.

My father wouldn't allow me to sleep on the alkali flat where all the other cowboys, Kent, Keith, and Warner slept. He had my bedroll laid out on a board inside the sheep wagon that was earlier used as a table. I was happy to go to sleep. Four o'clock in the morning came mighty early.

After three long days, we made it to the Hagerty Ranch, a small place with a house and a fenced meadow. Several cowboys continued pushing the cattle higher into the mountains the next day where they would graze all summer and the calves could fatten up for sale in November or December. The other riders rode back to the flat to pick up calves that had not made it to the mountain the day before. Calves will always return to the place where they were last "mothered up" which was where we had "nooned" the day before. The rest of that day was spent herding these calves and their mothers back to the mountains. We picked up stray "dry" cows from the first drive made the week before.

The first year I went on the roundup, for some reason, my dad decided he and I should ride back to Sunnyside the same night that we got to Hagerty Ranch. With a full moon lighting our way, he and I rode in silence for hours and hours over several mountain ranges through trees and brush and over cliffs and rocks. Sometimes I clung to the saddle horn with both hands as my horse seemed to disappear from under me when we dropped straight down the side of a mountain. When the moon went behind a cloud, I'd look down and to either side of me and see nothing but darkness. I heard only the horses breathing, their hooves on the rocks, and an occasional coyote howling. I think I was a little scared, but I never told my dad.

After we cleared the mountains and the riding got easier, my dad began to sing; he sang every song he knew. Daddy used to copy and memorize the words to songs (mostly cowboy songs) that he'd heard and loved. I knew some of the words to some of the songs, so I sang along with him. "Oh Bury Me Not on the Lone Prairie," "Cattle Call," "Red River Valley" were a few of the many, many songs we sang as we rode through the night. His absolute favorite song which he told me was also Uncle Murray's favorite was "The Strawberry Roan." He knew all the lyrics to that song which he sang as we rode along:

The Strawberry Roan

I was hangin' 'round town, just spendin' my time
Out of a job, not earnin' a dime
A feller steps up and he says, "I suppose
You're a bronc buster from the looks of your clothes."
"You figures me right, I'm a good one," I claim
"Do you happen to have any bad ones to tame?"
Said, "He's got one, a bad one to buck
At throwin' good riders, he's had lots of luck."

I gets all het up, and I ask what he pays
To ride this old nag for a couple of days
He offered me ten; I said, "I'm your man.
A broc never lived that I couldn't span."
He said, "Get your saddle, I'll give you a chance."
In his buckboard we hopped, and he drives to the ranch
I stayed 'til mornin' and right after chuck
I stepped out to see if this outlaw can buck.

Down in the horse corral standin' alone
Is an old Caballo, a Strawberry Roan
His legs are all spavined; he's got pigeon toes
Little pin eyes and a big Roman nose
Little pin ears that touched at the tip
A big 44 brand was on his left hip
U-necked and old, with a long lower jaw
I could see with one eye, he's a regular outlaw.

I gets the blinds on 'im, and it sure is a fright
Next comes the saddle, and I screws it down tight

113

Then I steps on 'im, and I raises the blinds
Get outta the way, boys, he's gonna unwind
He sure is a frog-walker, he heaves a big sigh
He only lacks wings, for to be on the fly
He turns his old belly right up to the sun
He sure is a sun-fishin' son of a gun.

He's about the worst bucker I've seen on the range
He'll turn on a nickel and give you some change
He hits on all fours and goes up on high
Leaves me a spinnin' up there in the sky
I turns over twice, and I comes back to earth
I lights in a cussin' the day of his birth.

I know there are ponies that I cannot ride
There's some of them left, they haven't all died.
I'll bet all my money, the man ain't alive
That'll stay with Old Strawberry
When he makes his high dive.

I was a very tired little girl when we got home just at daybreak, but looking back on that night, I realize it was one of the most perfect experiences of my life.

After several days in Cave Valley pushing the cattle farther north, all the cowboys showed up at Sunnyside. Counting the regular hired men on the ranch and the cow hands, Mom prepared a meal for at least twenty men. I don't think she knew exactly the day they would be showing up, but somehow she always had a huge roast, mashed potatoes, gravy, loaves of homemade bread, and several pies or a cake and homemade ice cream ready for them. Everybody within a hundred miles remembered my mother's meals.

My days as a cowhand were short-lived because at age eight I was old enough to be of help to my mother, and I didn't get to go on the cattle drives anymore. Now I would help my mother cook and pack hot meals to the cowboys. We'd drive the old truck to the approximate place on the white sage flat above the clump of cedars where we estimated they would be about noon and watch for the huge dust that stretched out for miles and miles.

The men then took turns watching the herd, mothering up the calves, and coming to eat as we spread all the food out on a canvas tarp. The truck was our only shade as dust blew into our eyes and mouths and onto our food, but nobody complained. The cowboys filled up on chili beans or mulligan stew, hot rolls, homemade applesauce, and sheet cake. They stretched their legs and leaned against the truck or a sage bush as they ate from tin plates and drank strong, hot coffee from tin cups. They relaxed, and they visited.

"That old bald-faced cow fell back again today. She's slower than most of the calves."

"We're making pretty good time though. We should get to Shingle Springs before dark."

"I chased a calf clean across the alkali flat before I got him turned."

I watched with envy as the men climbed back on their horses and started back to the cattle. After the men who had been holding the herd came in to eat, my mother and I gathered up the food and the kettles and dishes and headed back to the ranch. We had pots and pans to soak and clean and an evening meal to prepare for the hired men back at the ranch. Every year, I never stopped wishing I could climb on my horse and ride off with those cowboys.

Sally Jo & Lila

My life as a cow hand

20 Sunnyside School District

Starting first grade seemed scary to me, but surely Warner would take care of me, for he'd already gotten to second grade. That fall, there were to be three other kids riding up from the bottom meadows on their horse starting school with us. The teacher, Karma Reid, had already arrived on the mail truck from Lund, thirty-five miles away and had moved into the "teacher room," (a small room Daddy and Ed had built off the back of the bunkhouse). The schoolroom had been set up some time before in the empty house my grandparents had lived in. Desks and books from the Cave Valley School District had been placed in the living room, and there was an outhouse not far from the kitchen door. Everything was set, but I had no idea what a project it had been for my parents to get this school opened. First, the law required that small one-room schools must have five students to open. There were only three children to be found within thirty miles.

Then one day we thought we saw a wagon and some people down below the ranch. Sure enough, they were setting up camp. Daddy saddled his horse and rode to the lower meadow to talk with them, and he came back to report that this was a family who was "down and out." He had hired the father to help finish the haying and then announced that there were three school-age children. This was like a miracle for us; we now had our school. The kids were only in school for two short weeks, however. Their camping on our property was a lucky break for us, but it turned out to be the downfall of that family.

One late afternoon we noticed a dust far in the distance, indicating that a car was coming. It stopped at our ranch, and two dusty but important-looking men got out. They asked my dad if he had seen a family with a wagon and two horses come by. "Yes, they were down there," my dad said, pointing toward the lower field. The year was 1944, and we learned the man was a draft dodger. He had managed to stay hidden until then when, ironically, he was found in one of the most isolated spots in the state of Nevada—our ranch.

The father was taken away. The mother and her children started east to Pioche on the two horses. We drove out to find them and to offer them help, but the mother angrily announced that she needed no help from anyone. We drove home feeling like the whole situation was somehow our fault. Still, we did have five students on the roles, and our school was now officially opened.

Another rule about one-room schools in the '40s was that there must be three students to keep the school open. Bucky Riordan was that third student. He lived on a neighboring ranch twelve miles away and was sent to board with us during the weekdays. He only did that for a short time because he got very homesick. I think my brother and I were not very kind to him. Warner got him down and washed his face with snow more than once. We had seen so few other children that we found him strange. He walked pigeon-toed, and he used long words that we'd never even heard of. His mother drove to the ranch on Mondays to get the work which he would do during the week. She would bring it back the next Monday and pick up new assignments. His name remained on our school roster.

It turned out that I was a pretty good student. The fact that I had heard the entire curriculum before didn't hurt. My mother had taught Warner first grade at home the year before. She even taught our cousin, Orvis Tilby, for a short time. His mother, our Aunt Ruth, came to stay with us so she could get away from her abusive husband. Warner was not interested in learning anything that did not concern cows or machinery, and he and Orvis would take off running through the brush when Mom called them to come in for school. But I was a receptive student then, so I listened and learned. I even tried to coax Warner into listening and learning because I was afraid he would be sent back to the Ely school.

Warner and I had been separated for a short time the previous fall when he was boarded with Aunt Jo to attend first grade in Ely. Warner had hated Ely, and one Friday afternoon before Mom came to pick him up, Warner carried all his books to the teacher's desk, set them down, and announced that he would not be coming back. He told my mother and aunt what he had done, and he absolutely refused to ever go to school in Ely again. Mom then brought him home and arranged to homeschool him on the ranch through first grade. She got books and help from the State Department of Education under the supervision of Donald K. Perry, State Superintendent.

Soon Aunt Ruth and Orvis left. Orvis was not put in school again until he was eight years old when he had to start first grade again because his mother, my Aunt Ruth, "forgot" to enroll him in school. Warner did pass the first grade, and now we were both off to school together at the Sunnyside School District.

Ms. Reid was not a certified teacher at the time. She had gone to the University of Nevada in Reno for a short time, but had come back to Lund. Still, she was more qualified than anyone else within traveling distance, and she was hired. Our recesses got extended quite often while Warner and I spent time out playing in a big tree by the creek or over at Jackson Spring a mile and a half mile away. There was an old cellar there and more trees to climb.

Long before school even started each day Warner and I were out playing. Our favorite before-school game was walking on huge fallen cottonwood trees that covered a large lot. My father had cut them all down because they took water he needed to grow alfalfa. In this game, the trees were highways of our world. "Follow that tree around to the left," Warner would say, "and then go right, and you'll come to Reno. On the way back take another right, and you'll be in Pioche." Our cities were names we had heard mentioned by people at the ranch. Lund, Ely, Pioche, Sharp, Reno (an aunt lived there), Hiko, Alamo, New Mexico (not a city, but we didn't know that, where another aunt lived), Hagerty, Caliente, Pony Springs. Eventually we would hear our mother calling, "Sally, time to get your hair combed. Warner, get the fire built." By 9:00 the rats were all out of my hair, and our school building was toasty warm for the two students and the teacher.

I made new friends when Dick, Jane, Sally, and Spot appeared in my first grade reader. I could read this book perfectly, but I might have had the book memorized because there were so few books for me to read. I loved my teacher, and I cried when Ms. Reid rode the mail truck back to Lund for the last time that spring. Because of the before- and after-school games and my love for Ms. Reid, my first year passed quickly. Warner and I were now in second and third grades.

Probably because there was now an official school, two families with kids moved to the Hendrix ranch three miles away. A small white one-room building was moved onto our ranch from Cave Valley and two students, along with the teacher, rode their horses to our school each morning. The teacher was Alice Hendrix, the new bride of Clay Hendrix, who had moved back on the Hendrix ranch. Warner and I were the youngest students; the other two were in seventh and eighth grades. I liked school but I liked playing our before-school games with Warner better. I was never ready to stop playing.

Aunt Jo came to live with us and teach us the next year. Warner and I were again the only students with Bucky Riordan still on the school roster but getting homeschooled. I'm sure my parents were desperate to find a teacher because Aunt Jo lived at Hiko, a ranch seventy-five miles away, and my uncle would come and get her each weekend. This must have been a great sacrifice for her to leave her family and come help us out. But that was something our Aunt Jo would do. She had only one child, Elwood, who was ten years older than we were. He spent every summer on our ranch working for my dad from age thirteen to seventeen. He was like my older brother, and I adored him.

I only remember one day of the week that school year—Friday. Every Friday was craft day, and we got to work on *the dollhouse*. We walked to Daddy's shop, and Warner sawed boards and built a two-story house. Aunt Jo collected old pieces of linoleum and wallpaper as well as leftover paint and varnish, and I began to decorate the interior. Warner built furniture out of lathe and tin. Friday was the only day we could work on our house, and sometimes I had trouble sleeping on Thursday nights because I was so excited.

We finished the dollhouse about the same time we finished our third and fourth grades. How would our parents ever find someone to teach Warner and me the next year? Enter Gussie Ross.

Teacher Karma Reid and Sally Jo

21 Gussie Ross

Gussie Ross was the only applicant to apply for the teaching job when our parents notified the Nye County School District that we needed a teacher. We were sure she'd been blackballed out of every school district in Nevada when she accepted the job at the Sunnyside School District. She drove her little black model A over nine summits from Reno to Ely and then over Murry summit to Lund and thirty-five miles of rutted gravel road to get to her new job. Her greatest fear was that she would die out there, and we would bury her on the alkali flats. Warner and I did not like anything about her. She was old, and she always wore a scarf on her head, long white stockings, white high top shoes, and her favorite thing to say was, "Bloo blaa." Warner and I once told her that we had already dug her grave, and it was right in the middle of the alkali flat. She insisted that Warner back her car up three turns of the wheels and then forward two turns about every month so that the tires would not rot.

I think back now and realize what a horrible year that must have been for that poor old lady. What circumstances would have forced her to take such a job so far away from civilization? She boarded in the little teacher room off the back of the bunkhouse and of course ate her meals with us. She had all the answers when it came to home, marriage, and children although we were pretty sure she had never been married or had children. She probably had never even had a home. She was very displeasing to my mother.

Bucky Riordan's parents got a divorce and sold their ranch to the Eldridges. Tommy Eldridge was in the first grade. I spent most of my fourth-grade year sitting on the south side of the school building on a cement step teaching him to read. That was the forerunner to cooperative learning and maybe to my becoming a teacher. George was in the fifth grade with Warner, and then there were Donna Mae and Donald Dee who were in the seventh and eighth grade. A kitchen table was moved in for Donald Dee because he did not fit in the other desks which had attached chairs and lift-up lids.

Donald Dee drove his siblings the twelve miles to school each day in an old truck. Donna Mae and I spent our recesses by the spring above the school building. We sat in the huge old tree, and she read to me. There were so few books in our library that she reread some of the books. She read me *Just David* twice that year. Since then, I have probably reread that book four more times. *Just David* is about a world-famous musician whose wife died. He took his son, David, away from civilization and taught him to love music and play the violin. Then he died, and David came back to people for help. The family who found him in their barn belonged to a religion which would not allow dancing or singing or music. David said, "Your God must be different from mine because my God loves music." After many years his musical talent was discovered, and the world learned who his father was and what had happened to him. I hoped someday I would have a son who I could name David. I do have a son, David Warner, who is a gifted artist.

Gussie Ross was part of a surprise birthday party in December of that year when I turned nine. My mother decided I needed to be familiar with other children because I had seen so few in my life. There were never any little girls on the other ranches in the valley. There was no church or neighbors or classmates. My entire life revolved around the few people and the lives they led on our cattle ranch. Mom went to Lund where my Aunt Beulah helped her invite the friends of my cousins, Tommy and Lois, to my party.

After an early supper, Gussie Ross called me to her little room behind the bunkhouse. She told me she had a gift for my birthday, but it was hidden, and I had to search for it. After many hints and "bloo, blahs," I soon found a small plastic ring. Somehow she managed to keep me occupied until my mother called for me to come back to the house. It was cold and dark, so I ran the short distance to the kitchen door. I was excited to show my mother the plastic ring. Just as I ran up the step to the dining room, huge amounts of children jumped out at me and yelled, "Surprise!"

I had never been so frightened in my life. Rattlesnakes could have sprung out at me, and I would not have been as scared. I'd never seen that many children in my life, and I did not recognize a single one of them. I began to scream and then to cry. My brother opened my presents, my mother cut the cake, and everyone sang "Happy Birthday" to me. I, however, did not stop crying for the entire two hours. The children climbed back into the car that had earlier coasted quietly off the road and stopped above the front gate. They were then driven the long way home. There had probably been five or six children, but for me, there might as well have been a thousand. I probably should have been introduced to the world of children one child at a time.

Warner and I left the Sunnyside School District in 1948. The year with Gussie Ross caused my mother to say, "Enough," for she refused to speculate on what kind of teacher might show up to teach us the next year.

The small white school building was moved to the Hendrix Ranch the year after we left and then to the ranch twelve miles away the following year. The three ranchers within the boundaries of the Sunnyside School District took turns moving the little school building to their ranch, causing it to be called the Revolving School District. In the mid-1950s, one-room schools were consolidated during the Eisenhower Administration. Teachers were no longer paid by the state to teach as few as three children in those isolated places. I think I remember seeing remnants of desks and books in the dump above the ranch in the late '50s, but I still have a special book, *Just David*, and it is stamped, "Property of Sunnyside School District."

REPORT OF *Daily Jo Ann Tupple*

Sunnyside Dist, Lund Nev Public School

Sept 15, to , 19 47 - 19 48

ATTENDANCE DEPORTMENT SCHOLARSHIP	1st Mo.	2d Mo.	3d Mo.	4th Mo.	5th Mo.	6th Mo.	7th Mo.	8th Mo.	9th Mo.	10th Mo.	Class Standing	Examination	AVERAGE
Days Present	16	19	17	16	18	20	19	17	20				
Days Absent	0		1	1	0	0	0	0	0				
Times Tardy	0	0	0	0	0	0	0	0	0				
Deportment	B+	a	a-	a	a-	a	a	a-	a				
STUDIES													
Reading	a	a	a	a	a	a	a	a	a				
Phonics													
Spelling	B+	a-	a	a	a	a	a	a	a				
Writing	B	a-	a	a	a	a	a	a	a				
Language	B	a-	a	a	a	a+	a	a	a				
History		a-	a	a	a	a	a	a	a				
Geography	B	a-	a-	a	a	a	a	a	a				
Written Arith.	B	a-	a	a	a	a	a	a	a				
Mental Arith.	B-	a	a-	a	a	a	a	a	a				
Music	B	a	a	a	a	a	a	a	a				
Drawing	a	a	a	a	a	a	a	a	a				
Hygiene *Health*		a	a	a	a	a	a	a					
Civics													
Business Forms													
Current Events													
Manual Training													
~~Domestic~~ Science		a	a	a	a	a							

Jessie M. Rice

Teacher.

). ✓—Armanko Office Supply Co. Reno, Nevada.

Fourth grade report card

22 Short-Lived Excitement

When Gussie Ross pulled out of the yard in her little black "fliver" at the end of Warner's and my fourth and fifth grades, my parents made a decision that would change my life forever. They decided schooling Warner and me on the ranch was no longer an option. My parents decided to buy a house in Ely where Mother, Warner, Bonnie, and I would live during the week. I had been to Ely so few times I could remember every trip, so the thought of living there seemed daunting and scary to me. Daddy knew I was not going to be happy with their decision. He couldn't even get me to go to town for a day—let alone live there. "Sally is going to miss the ranch more than anyone else," Grandma Famie told my parents. She was right, but she seemed to be the only one to understand that.

Daddy explained that he and Mom would be going to Salt Lake City to buy furniture for every room in the new house. I would have my own bedroom with a brand-new bedroom set. I couldn't help but get a little excited to be going to a "real" school. I'd asked for a bed with a bookcase headboard and a vanity with a big mirror and matching stool. My mother and I sat with the *Sears Roebuck and Montgomery Ward* catalogs looking for school clothes. I would be needing to wear dresses, she told me.

My excitement was short-lived. I can only remember three things I liked about Ely. A clump of brush on the hill above our house where I built a fort and went to hide out, Mrs. Pavolakis's donut shop, and the post office where I was allowed to drive down the back street each evening after supper to pick up the mail.

I later learned I was considered a rich kid when we moved to Ely because our house was up on the Hill. I had thought the girls with the Jansen sweaters were the rich kids. Our house was on the street where doctors and business people lived which might explain my father's reason for buying that house. He was a successful rancher then and probably wanted everyone to know it. I can't think of any other reason for my parents to buy that particular house. The houses on that street were next to the mountain on the west side of town, and they had basements backed into the hill. Warner's and my bedrooms were underground. I could just barely see a tiny slice of daylight above a concrete box outside my window. A dark, dank tunnel outside my bedroom door led to the garage. Moisture seeped through outcroppings of rock and clay in the walls of the tunnel. I was sick the entire time I lived in that house—probably from mold.

Other rooms in the basement were the small room just big enough for our freezer, and the washroom—with a toilet, a washer and dryer, and a mangle. The coal bin and furnace were on the back side of the house next to my bedroom. Steep wooden steps led up to the kitchen, bathroom, my parent's bedroom, and a large living room. Daddy had an office off the living room with a view of the mountain. A brick wall kept the house and yard from falling down the hill. To visit us, one parked on the street and walked up a steep flight of rock steps to our front door.

I only had my bedroom to myself for one year until Bonnie could be moved from her crib upstairs in the master bedroom to the other twin bed downstairs in my room. Bonnie was afraid to sleep in the basement alone, so I had to have the same bedtime as my three-year-old sister when I was almost twelve. I hated Ely, I hated school, but mostly, I hated that house. I went from sleeping outside almost every night of my life on the ranch to sleeping in a dungeon. *In every way*, I thought, *I've gone from the light to the dark.*

I always wished Daddy would have bought a house in Lund, which was thirty miles closer, and the school was smaller. Daddy explained that he did all his shopping and banking in Ely—not Lund, so it made more sense to live in Ely. Nothing I had ever learned or done prepared me for Ely. Truthfully, I was way out of my comfort zone. The world made more sense to me when I lived where I knew what was expected of me. I felt I was just passing time in Ely. Life on the ranch, where I had value working beside my mother, father, and brother and caring for my animals, was my real life.

I remember how I hated not having any chores. I wasn't expected to do anything. On the ranch, I helped my parents with all the things that needed to be done every day. In Ely, my mom was able to get everything done with the help of a cleaning lady. I remember seeing Jeanne Stevenson walking home with a bag of groceries. How I wished my mother would send me to the grocery store for her. I felt so useless. At least Warner had one chore. He was expected to shovel coal from the bin into the furnace every day.

Warner learned very quickly that it was not cool to have his sister be his friend. He made friends with Bobby and Jerry Stever down the street and was at their house most of the time. During the week, when we were living in Ely, Warner couldn't be bothered with me at all. He needed to be home for supper; other than that, he spent all his time at the Stever's house, and he ignored me completely. My life got even worse when I became the target of a vicious little gang of girls. These girls would jump out of line when I walked toward them. They wouldn't sit on the same swing seat where I'd been sitting. "Cooties," they'd scream and then run away.

I lived for Fridays when I would run all the way home because I knew Mom would be waiting to take us back to the ranch. I missed my dad terribly as well as my horse Flicka, dogs, cats, lambs, and my pet hen Maggie. Every Friday afternoon we'd load our car with things that needed to go to the ranch and then make the hour and a half trip. After I called Flicka and brought her from the pasture to the house, Mom and I would start dinner for my dad and the hired men. Since they'd been "batching it" all week, she'd deal with burned pans and a very dirty kitchen. The fridge was always filled with cans and buckets of cream that I spent several hours on Saturday mornings churning. Mom baked three loaves of bread and made a pot of soup or beans for the men to eat the following week. l

I'd wake up Sunday mornings with a sinking feeling that just got worse as the day went on knowing we'd be going back to town late that afternoon. It was always a fight getting Warner and me into the car for the drive back to Ely. Mom started timing our trips back at the same time as *Our Miss Brooks, Jack Benny,* and *The Life of Riley* were on the car radio. She also bribed us by letting us take turns driving until we got to Murry Summit just outside of Ely.

Daddy sat Warner and me down and gave us a talk about living in Ely. It was good for us to learn to live off the ranch, he said. "Very soon you two kids will adjust just fine to city life."

First Christmas in Ely, 1948

Ely house, 811 Pine St.

Part Two

The Socialization of Sally

23 *The Socialization of Sally*

A bell rang, and hoards of noisy children tramped up the stairs of the old brick school building into the classroom where I was sitting. I didn't know there were that many kids in the whole world, and every one of them were staring straight at me. My first day at the Ely Grade School had just begun.

Mom had brought Warner and me to meet our teachers earlier that morning. "This is Sally Whipple," my mother said to Mrs. Hughes. "She's been going to a one-room school at the Sunnyside Ranch until now." Mrs. Hughes assured my mother that I would enjoy fifth grade at the public school, and I'd be just fine. Mom then took Warner to meet his sixth-grade teacher.

I was so scared that when the teacher asked me to stand and introduce myself, I couldn't speak. Mrs. Hughes told the class my name and explained that I'd never been to a public school before. Then she added, "Sally must have gotten plenty of sunshine at Sunnyside because I've never seen such yellow hair." I crouched in my seat, but I couldn't think of any way to hide my head or my hair.

The next day I refused to go to school. Warner said he was not going back either, but my mother made us both get into the car, and she drove us to school and deposited us onto the playground where we promptly headed up the mountain behind the school and walked the railroad tracks until school was out.

The following day, we did the same thing. On the third day, my mother found out and walked each of us to our classrooms where the teachers met us. She continued to do that until we both swore on a stack of Bibles that we'd not skip school again. We stayed in school after that, but when we got our first report cards, Warner and I had sixteen Fs between the two of us. How could this be when we were straight A students at the Sunnyside School District?

I hated Beth Campbell (I have no idea why), and she didn't like me either. We went down to the bottom of the outside basement steps and fought every recess. Kids leaned on the railing above and cheered us on. All the new dresses my mother has gotten me for school got ripped up. There were holes where my sashes had been.

I didn't like Morris Grubb either. He annoyed Jeanne Stevenson too, so she and I waited for him by the Episcopal Church after school. Jeanne stood at the edge of a hill. I dared him to push Jeanne down the hill. She stepped aside, and he took a nosedive down the hill; he began to cry. We didn't have any more trouble with Morris Grubb.

Finally I heard about something fun in school. I rushed home one day to ask my mother to buy me a baton. "A teacher is going to teach baton lessons after school," I told her, excitedly. Mom was equally excited to think I had found something I might enjoy about school and bought me a baton that very night. I loved my new baton, and I practiced twirling it and throwing it into the air every day. I also took it to school and whacked anybody who bothered me. Dickey Bell tried to kiss me, and I whacked him. Diane Marshall wouldn't let me get to my locker; I whacked her. I whacked Sheridan McConnell when she told me I should learn how to behave. The principal called my mom and told her I was not to bring my baton to school anymore. I was furious. I hated that school.

I sat on the office floor almost every night after school. I got four nights for spitting pine nut shells across the room, and then I got four more nights for running across the tops of Mrs. McGregor's desks in math class. At least once a week, I accumulated another few nights on the office floor as punishment for some behavior. There were rarely any girls on the office floor—just boys. A teacher, Mrs. Klein, stood in front of me with her hands on her hips. "Sally, aren't you ashamed to be sitting here every night after school? This is not something a lady does." I didn't care what a lady does. I felt like hitting the next person who told me I'm supposed to be a lady.

My mother never got mad at me for staying after school. Her philosophy was if I chose to sit on the office floor after school, that was my choice. We all have choices. When I'd get home, she was waiting to ask me how my day had gone. I'd answer, "How many more days until Friday?" Daddy didn't know I got into trouble at school because he didn't live with us in Ely. That was a good thing because my dad didn't necessarily believe in Mom's choice theory. I was the perfect child when I was on the ranch.

Finally I graduated from the Ely Grade School. I stopped by the office to ask the principal if I needed to come back next year to serve out the rest of my days on the office floor. He told me I definitely did **not** need to come back next year for any reason. Maybe he wasn't such a bad guy after all, I decided.

At White Pine High School, my first period class was sociology with Mr. Tripp who was a fat jolly fellow with scabs on his bald head and mismatched socks. "Sally Whipple," he began calling names from his roll sheet. He stopped and looked up. "Who is Sally Whipple? Raise your hand please." I did. "I just wondered what you look like. I've been hearing about you for two years." That was one of few times I remember being famous.

Sociology wasn't my favorite subject. (Actually, I didn't have a favorite subject. I knew how to ride a horse and drive a tractor, so there really wasn't anything else I cared to learn). The major project for Mr. Tripp's class was to create a vocational notebook. We were to do research on the education and experience we would need to become who we wanted to be when we grew up. Our final project was to turn in a book with text and pictures. Mr. Tripp would not let me write my book on what I wanted to be. I either wanted to be a cowgirl and a horse trainer or to drive heavy equipment or big cattle trucks.

"For example," Mr. Tripp said (probably for my benefit), "girls will not write their books on welding." A few kids laughed at his joke. I did not. I raised my hand and asked, "What if a girl wants to become a welder? Why can't she write her book on welding?" The whole class broke up with laughter like they thought I was trying to be funny. They didn't understand that welding was something I'd always wanted to learn to do. I finally gave up and did my book on interior decorating. At least that was acceptable to everybody. I realized it was kind of neat to make people laugh, though, so from then on I decided to make sure the kids in all my classes had a good time. My conduct grades were never the same again.

All my friends got to stay home one day at the end of the school year because they'd earned good grades. My grades were okay, but there was always a catch to everything. We didn't get a special day if we got a D or F in conduct. Mom told me she was sorry I had to go to school, but I must understand when I don't follow the rules, I have to pay the price.

"I understand," I said to my mother as I left our house. I stopped by Mrs. Pavalakos's bakery on the way to school because Mom gave me money to buy donuts for my first-period class. The whole day turned out to be great fun. Most of the kids who had to come back were boys, and they were always more fun anyway.

The truth was school in Ely had turned out not to be such a bad thing. By the time I was a senior, I was the treasurer of my senior class, treasurer of the Bo-ca-baks (the school pep club), secretary of the student body, and I was voted the wittiest girl at White Pine High School. I even got chosen to go to Girl's State. When I decided in Mr. Tripp's class my freshman year of high school to make everyone laugh, I found the key to having many friends. My mother kept telling me things would turn out for the best, and I guess she was right. I can't imagine how I would have turned out if I had continued going to school on the ranch. Although some might dispute this, I believe I did become somewhat socialized when I moved to Ely. Daddy was not completely right, though, when he told me I'd get used to city life. I've always known I would have been happier living a ranch life.

High school friends: Karen, Barbara, Nola, Sally, Jeanne

Wittiest

DON WILHOITE AND SALLY WHIPPLE

Sally voted wittiest at White Pine High School

Sally (in front) with friends at Ely Grade School / 1949

24 *The Hardest Winter in Our History*

Seventy-mile-an-hour winds and temperatures hovering at zero degrees or below for almost four months made the winter of 1948-1949 the hardest winter in Eastern and Southeastern Nevada's history. It was the coldest ever recorded in Nevada. It began snowing on December 2 and did not stop until March.

That same winter, my Mom, Warner, Bonnie, and I moved to Ely for school. I missed the ranch terribly and lived for Fridays when we went back to the ranch and I could see my dad and my animals. However, on December of that first winter, the weather and roads got so bad, Mom couldn't drive us to the ranch on the weekends, and Daddy did not come to Ely until Christmas.

By New Years, as the blizzards and freezing temperatures continued, my dad knew he was in trouble. He had to get back to the ranch, gather his cattle off the open range, and get them to feed. On January 3, he left for the ranch. His best friend since high school, Shirley Brown, went along to help save his cattle. We did not see them again until March.

Shortly after my dad left Ely, President Truman declared Eastern and Southeastern Nevada a disaster area. State, county, and federal agencies worked together to open roads and haul feed and water to stranded livestock. Sixteen C-82 flying boxcars from McChord Air Field in Washington State began flying hay to the Ely airport on January 24. The bales were then loaded onto army national guard trucks, but most of the time they could not get through the drifting snow on any roads out of Ely. The ranchers could not get their sheep and cattle out to the roads anyway. Something had to be done quickly or that part of Nevada would be a total economic disaster.

That was when the pilots of the flying boxcars began making air drops directly to the starving herds. Local ranchers rode in the planes to help locate stranded cattle and sheep and sometimes to serve as "pushers." Men with ropes tied around their waists were stationed at the tails of the planes near an open door. Pilots flew two hundred feet from the ground and when the rancher yelled, "Drop," the "pushers" shoved the bales out the door. This worked very well except in a few instances. One bale "bombed" a sheep herder's donkey, killing it instantly, then bounced fifteen feet killing his other donkey as well. Another bale went through a rancher's new washhouse, destroying his brand-new washing machine.

People were swarming everywhere in Ely that winter of 1949 which made living in town even more scary for me. News people from all over the country were there. The Hotel Nevada and the motels were all filled as well as every restaurant. Transport planes were landing and taking off constantly. One afternoon on my way home from school, I walked by a street lined with army military vehicles. The drivers were standing beside their trucks and most of them were African-American. The only time I'd ever seen a black person was in a book called *Little Black Sambo*. I ran all the way home and was almost too breathless to describe to my mother what I had just seen.

I was too young to understand all that was going on, but I knew the weather was terrible, and I knew planes were droning overhead; and the army trucks had something to do with my dad needing to be gone for weeks without us even hearing from him. Mom was very worried about my dad, but she also worried that we would lose all our cattle and would be out of the ranching business. She heard that thirty-five thousand head of cattle were marooned in White Pine, Nye, and Lincoln counties. She had no idea how bad it was for my dad.

Dad and Shirley worked for ten weeks, almost day and night, to save our cattle. When they had gotten to the ranch that first week of January, they realized the road south to the open range was completely drifted over. It was much worse than my dad had thought. Somehow he had to get feed to his cattle. For three days, he and Shirley worked at starting a small International TD9 crawler tractor my dad had bought the previous summer. He figured when he got time to work on it, he could probably use it on the ranch. It turned out that little tractor saved the ranch.

Finally after draining the oil and heating it, they got it running. They loaded the cattle truck with bales of hay, hooked the sheep wagon behind the truck, and with a couple of cowboys Daddy had hired, they began the journey to save the snowbound cattle. My dad went ahead with the caterpillar pushing a snowplow. The snowdrifts were so deep and heavy that he needed to back up and take a run at them every few yards. Shirley came behind with the truck and sheep wagon. If he waited five minutes too long, high winds drifted the road closed again.

They were finally able to get to the sink of White River Valley where most of Daddy's cattle were "wintering." Cattle were huddled together in piles to keep from freezing to death. The cowboys rode out and kicked cows out of the piles, dropped some bales of hay, and continued on. The two men on horseback rode in opposite directions looking for more piles of cattle. Day after day they frantically worked, stopping only to warm up in the sheep wagon and to eat and sleep a few hours. Miraculously, the truck and the caterpillar started right up every morning.

By the time they got to Rye Patch, they were completely out of supplies, so the next morning, they went back to the ranch. After loading the truck with fifty-gallon barrels of water and gasoline as well as any food supplies they found at the ranch, they started back. It was still snowing hard, and the temperature was far below zero when, at four o'clock in the afternoon, they got stuck just past the gap. High winds and blowing snow made it impossible for them to go in any direction. They sat in the truck the rest of that day and throughout the night starting the truck to run the heater only when they got so cold they couldn't stand it. My dad said that was the closest he ever came to freezing to death.

The plan was to gather as many cattle as Dad had feed for and move them to the ranch. Ed Rowlie would feed them there. They would then drive the rest of the cattle sixty miles south to Hiko where my dad could get hay shipped in from Imperial Valley, California, to feed them through the winter. Daddy had no way of knowing the details of the Hay Lift or how big a disaster other ranchers were facing, but he saw huge flying boxcars circling low overhead and then watched as bales of hay dropped from the sky to feed cattle he was not able to reach.

Almost two months later, they had as many cows as they could find moved to Hiko. He was able to contact my mom on a forest service radio in early March to tell her he was okay. He and Shirley returned to Ely a few weeks later. When Daddy tapped on the back door of our house late one night, my mother thought she was looking at a very thin dark-skinned full-bearded beggar, so she woke Warner before realizing who he was.

My dad and Shirley stayed in town only long enough to rent an airplane and hire a pilot to fly them back over the entire sink, so they could spot cattle they had missed or any cows that were late calving. They then went back the second time with more hay.

By April, when he knew he had saved as many cattle as he could, my dad came to Ely to talk to the bank about a loan to pay for the hay and to save the ranch. The bank in Ely readily lent money to the ranchers. "I know them all," Gordon Lathrop, the president of the bank, said, "they'll pay me back when they can."

It took many years to get out of debt after that horrible winter. Daddy never was able to run as many cattle again. Our herd dropped from three thousand head at one time to just eight hundred. In the history of Eastern Nevada, there never was a winter worse than 1948 and 1949 for the cattle and sheep ranchers. That winter, along with the extreme drought that followed, caused many sheep and cattle ranchers to go out of business. My dad was able to keep Sunnyside, but he never was as prosperous. The days of true open-range grazing were over.

When school was out in May 1949 and we'd moved back to the ranch, my mother, father, and I rode down through the sink of White River. I remember Daddy pointing out large dark spots in the distance and telling us they were piles of cattle worth thousands of dollars. Many of them did not freeze to death but suffocated trying to keep warm.

That winter, the first one I spent off the ranch, was also one of my personal worst winters. Warner and I got all the childhood diseases: measles, mumps, and chicken pox as we had never been around other children before. I had my tonsils out shortly after Christmas. The dentist found thirty-six cavities on my first visit as I'd never been to a dentist, and I started wearing thick glasses when the teacher realized I couldn't see the numbers on the blackboard. Mom said it was a miracle I made it through the fifth grade.

Mom probably had an even harder adjustment than I did. It was close to zero degrees most mornings, but she didn't think to buy me a coat until a neighbor of ours called. "I see Sally walking to school without a coat. She must be terribly cold." Mom was embarrassed; we went to Goodman Tidballs after school that afternoon to get me a brand-new winter coat. Not only did Mother have to learn city ways, but she had a two-year-old, an unhappy ten-year-old, and an eleven-year-old son who wasn't used to listening to his mother, let alone obeying her. She had to manage without Daddy who was gone the entire winter working to save Sunnyside. We were all glad when spring arrived that year. We had survived the terrible winter, and we were together again back on the ranch.

TD9 caterpillar that saved the ranch in 1949

Loading hay bales into C82 Flying Boxcars for hay drops

25 Hiko

I was allowed to drive down the wash to visit my cousin Kathryn Rose at Hiko when I was about twelve years old. The wash was seventy-five miles of washboard road, deep ruts, and washouts from Sunnyside south to Hiko. Each trip was different because we never knew when a flash flood would move down from the hills and take out parts of the road, forcing travelers to reroute. Usually, if there had been a huge washout, somebody who had come up the wash from the south would stop at the ranch and warn us.

"Watch for the Cold Springs turnoff; you'll have to take a sharp right for thirty yards or so before you can cross the washout and make it through. It's best to take a run at it," they might say. That was good advice because the road could disappear right in front of us. I always hoped I could stop in time or turn to the side and stop before I dove into a wash. Fortunately, I had been driving Daddy's old Ford truck since I was old enough to reach the pedals, so I always made it.

My cousins, Keith and Kent, who lived at Hiko, had their Sunnyside truck. This truck usually lasted about a year before the body fell off the frame or the axle broke. Their theory was that if they hit the washes going about fifty miles an hour, they would fly over them instead of diving into them. Many times I would catch a ride with my cousins to visit Kathryn instead of driving Dad's truck. With no seat belts, we would fly all over the inside of the cab, and the corduroy road kept us bouncing for the entire seventy-five miles. My dad didn't know about their theory, or he never would have allowed me to get in the truck with either one of them.

When I drove by myself, my parents insisted that I have a sack of jerky and a canteen of water, but I always added a peanut butter and jelly sandwich and a can of Vienna sausages. Mom and Dad counted on someone coming up the wash to report if I had broken down. No report, I had made it, according to them. I enjoyed seeing the bobcats, coyotes, and mustangs along the way; and I always stopped at the petroglyphs, all along the cliffs about three-fourths of the way to Hiko. I would eat my lunch and drink my water and imagine Indians riding and whooping, and then circling inside the natural rock corral where I sat.

Hiko is a ranch near the small Mormon community of Alamo. Maybe two hundred people lived in the whole area, but I might as well have been driving into a city when I compared it to Sunnyside. Usually I brought along a new dress that I'd ordered from the Sears catalog because they had Sundays and church at Hiko, which we did not have at Sunnyside.

I loved everything about going to church in Alamo. Getting ready was fun. We all took turns taking baths, and then we dressed up in our church clothes. I never remembered taking a bath for a special occasion before. Then Keith, Kent, Kathryn Rose, and their mother, Aunt Ouida, and I drove to Alamo. They knew all the people, and many of them conducted the service, gave talks, and entertained us. If I came to Hiko on the first Sunday of the month, people would get up and "bear their testimonies." I learned stories of their lives, their trials, as well as wonderful things that happened to them. I felt like each one of them was my friend. One young couple harmonized together at some of the sacrament meetings. Other times, members played the piano, guitar, violin, or groups of people sang; and we got to sing together. The service was always beautiful.

My ancestors on both sides are Mormon, but I joined the Mormon church because religion to me means the church in Alamo and all the wonderful people who live there. Whenever I go to a Mormon church anywhere in the world, those people are still there—different names, same people.

After church, we visited with church members and then drove back to Hiko where we had free time for the rest of the day. This too was exciting because not only did we not have Sundays or church at Sunnyside, we didn't have days off. Kathryn and I sometimes rode horses, or we floated on tubes down the wide cement ditch across the road from the house. Sometimes I would just sit in the living room and listen to Kathryn play the piano. We had all the daily chores to do—feeding chickens, gathering eggs, milking cows, cooking, doing dishes, watering, but we never started a new job on Sunday.

Saturday nights were fun too. A group of people would set up folding chairs on the tennis court behind the service station and garage in Alamo, and we would drive down to see a movie which they showed with a twelve-millimeter projector on a big screen put up at one end of the cement slab. Someone had to order the movie and pay for it, so we were charged a quarter to watch. Of course, anyone could sit off to the side, see the movie and not pay, but nobody would ever do that. They showed "Seven Brides for Seven Brothers" on two different Saturdays. I guess they thought as long as they already had the movie, why not watch it twice before they sent it back. A few times Keith drove us to Caliente fifty miles away for a movie at the theater. To me that was like seeing a Broadway show.

Looking back, I realize the real reason my father sent me to Hiko, and Kathryn was allowed to come to visit me, was so we could help our mothers with special jobs that needed to be done. I helped Aunt Ouida with the spring cleaning, and Kathryn helped Mom and I prepare for the family reunions every year. Kathryn and I would get up early and help with breakfast then do some baking. We'd do the milking (my mother would never allow me to milk cows at Sunnyside. She claimed I did enough work and if I once did it, I'd forever have that job too), feed the animals, do housework (usually spring cleaning) and yard work.

I came to Hiko two summers to take care of Kathryn and Kent while Aunt Ouida went to summer school for a few weeks at the University of Nevada in Reno. Keith was married and living close by, but I took my job very seriously and was determined to get Kent up every morning and to have breakfast for the three of us.

I loved the idea of a mail truck coming almost every day from Caliente. The mail man brought groceries and other items the people in Pahranagat Valley needed. I always had an order waiting for him; there was probably a year's supply of canned goods in the cupboard on the screen porch the first summer when Aunt Ouida got back home.

She must have thought I did a good job, though, because she wanted me back the next summer. Looking back, I find it interesting that I was "taking care of" Kent and Kathryn. Kent was the same age as I was, and Kathryn was two years younger. Aunt Ouida believed I was very responsible and competent. She'd always want me to do the driving when we took trips to Las Vegas or Caliente or even on one excursion to Boulder Dam.

As I got older I was able to stay away from home without getting homesick. I still worried about my mother who had all the ranch work to do as well as caring for my baby sister, but by then Bonnie had gotten a little older. I loved Hiko and Alamo and was always happy to head down the Wash whenever my father decided I could go help out again. That was the only time I would agree to leave Sunnyside.

Sally Jo and Kathryn Rose

Sally Jo and Kathryn Rose playing dolls at Hiko

Petroglyphs on road to Hiko

26   The Miracle of Music

I became aware of the peaceful, joyous feeling music brought to me when I was less than four years old. My mother and Dad sang songs as we made the long trip from Sunnyside to Hiko to see Uncle Murray and Aunt Ouida. Of course Daddy would always be at his happiest when he would be seeing his older brother, and I picked up on his moods as a very young girl. We drove to Hiko several times a year. I never knew anyone to love music like my dad. He knew the words to every song he'd ever heard and liked. Mom knew some of the words to some of the songs, "You Are My Sunshine," "Don't Fence Me In," "A Paper Doll to Call My Own," "Pistol Packin' Mama," "White Cliffs of Dover," and of course, my favorite (one I would sing with them), "Mares Eat Oats and Does eat Oats and Little Lambs Eat Ivey." Mother would harmonize with Daddy as we traveled down the wash. Their singing made the long drive go faster.

Music, truthfully, has always made everything go easier for me. Musical instruments touched my soul, and the stories told in cowboy songs gave me understanding and enlightenment about my thoughts and feelings when there was no one to talk to or no other sources to draw from. Words to classic country songs have paralleled my life. I was nurtured by old classic country songs, and it seems like most have been written with me in mind.

Almost everybody in Daddy's family was musical. Grandma Rose Ellen had a beautiful singing voice, as did my dad. Grandpa insisted that many of his girls learn to play the piano. Murray was the most gifted musician, playing many instruments. Daddy played the harmonica and sang. He also learned to play the accordion. At night they'd gather into the parlor and listen to the beautiful music coming from the piano rolls played on the very expensive player piano Grandpa gave to my grandmother.

I took piano lessons on that same player piano several decades later. Juanita Hendrix (wife of Findley), who moved to the ranch closest to ours, gave me lessons for a couple of years. The only time I knew my father would not ask me to run an errand or do a chore was when I was practicing the piano. I continued to take lessons after we moved to Ely when my parents bought a new piano for the Ely house. I learned to read music, but I never had a musical "gift" except I can yodel. When I was in the eighth grade, I had a dream that I could yodel. The next morning I realized I really could yodel.

I was always in awe of my Aunt Ruth when she played the piano "by ear." We could hum a tune to her, and she'd play it perfectly without ever learning to read music. I remember my mother laying down her dishrag to come into the small parlor at the ranch and sing with Ruth while she played.

Kathryn Rose (Murray's daughter) inherited her father's musical talent. She could play by ear, but her mother made great sacrifices to give her piano lessons in Las Vegas. She has perfect pitch which is a rare gift. I was never a sitting person, but I had no problem sitting while listening to Kathryn play for the hours she was required to practice. She could have been a concert pianist, but her dream was to be a nurse. She rarely plays the piano now (except when she comes to my house and plays on the same player piano given to our grandmother over one hundred years ago). The player part no longer works, but the piano resonates a more beautiful sound than any of the new pianos. I get it tuned every year, and I play for a few minutes at night before I go to sleep.

I got my first radio when I was about twelve years old. I lived for Saturday nights when I could listen to the *Grand Ole Opry*. I would plug my small green plastic radio into the one large 9-volt battery my dad would buy me each summer. When we went for our walks after supper on Saturday nights, I could not stand to miss one song, so I'd put the large battery and the radio in my red wagon and pull them along as we walked. Was this the original Walkman radio? After the walk, I would listen to my radio as I lay in my bedroll on the army cot that I moved all over the ranch. The problem was the *Grand Ole Opry* was from 7:00 p.m. until midnight. Many times I'd fall asleep and use up the battery attached to my radio, but as I lay tucked into my bedroll, the words and music of every song seemed to touch my soul. I couldn't stand to reach over and turn my radio knob to off when a song was playing.

The next morning, the radio was still on, and the battery was dead. I would cry and beg, but my father would not buy me another battery. Usually, Ed Rowlie would catch someone going to town and give them money to buy me a new battery. Finally, Daddy found me an alarm clock. I'd set it for midnight and when the alarm went off, I'd wake up and turn off my radio.

I was in my teens, when my parents found me a record player that worked on direct current. That meant that I had to start the water-powered generator to run my phonograph. I bought a Hank Williams 78 rpm record at the record store in Ely. Any afternoon that my dad was off the ranch, I'd run to pull the head gate, so the generator would start, and I could play my phonograph. (The water was needed for irrigating our alfalfa, so Daddy wouldn't have been happy if he'd known I rerouted the water during the day.) Then my mother and I would listen to Hank Williams over and over again as we worked together. She and I were scrubbing down the kitchen walls and ceiling one day. Hank began sorrowfully singing "I Can't Help It If I'm Still In Love with You." I said to my mother, "If I jilted somebody and he sang this song to me, I'd have to take him back." I remember Mother saying that it would be hard not to, but I should not marry somebody because I feel sorry for him. We'd start the generator at nights during the winter to have electric lights. I bought a new record whenever I got a little money, so I had a few more records to play in the evenings in my bedroom. Small 45 rpms were cheaper, but they had only one song on each side.

Every summer, the Whipple family came to the ranch for a family reunion. It took several men to haul the player piano onto the front lawn where everyone danced under the trees. My cousin Jack played a concertina that he brought home from the WWII. My dad played the harmonica and accordion, and we all sang and danced.

Daddy learned to play Eddie Arnolds's "Cattle Call" and many other cowboy songs on the accordion. He'd play "Put Your Little Foot" and "Oh, Johnny, Oh" on the harmonica while he and Mom danced around the kitchen. When eight-track tapes came out, he'd play them over and over until he memorized the words to the songs he loved. He'd recite or sing songs at all the functions in Lund.

I have a huge record—cassette and CD collection of old classic country music, folk songs, and even opera. I have a lifetime subscription to Sirus Satellite Radio, so now I am back to listening to the *Grand Ole Opry* every Saturday night. And I can listen to my CD player or my iPod day and night without worrying about pulling a head gate or falling asleep and having a dead battery when I wake up in the morning. It seems like a miracle that I can listen to music from morning to night whether I am at home, driving, or using earplugs connected to my iPod. Music touches me more deeply than any other thing in my life. It brings me joy when I'm sad, peace when I'm anxious, and hope when I'm discouraged. I can't imagine living without it.

Daddy playing accordion on front lawn

27 My Father's Daughter—A Lady?

It didn't matter to my father that I was raised on a ranch and loved everything about ranch life. He was determined that I was going to be a lady. I was ten years old when he caught me imitating Ted Gardner, a real old hardened cowboy, who worked for my dad and who was my idol. Daddy was furious.

I followed Ted around the ranch fascinated with everything he did. I even tried walking bowlegged and spitting. He was the person I admired most until I learned about Annie Oakley; she could shoot. Ted roped, broke wild horses, chewed tobacco, and smoked. What really made me stand in awe of him was that he rolled his own cigarettes with one hand. First he slid the cigarette paper out of his pocket with his forefinger and thumb. He held it to his mouth and licked both sides of it then held it on his tongue while he poured tobacco from a small cloth pouch marked Bull Durham. While he put the pouch back in his pocket, he rolled the cigarette with his very yellow teeth and his tongue. Next came the most exciting part and what got me in trouble. He struck the match on the leg of his Levi's to light the cigarette. One swipe and the match flared as he held it to the tobacco in the neatly rolled-up cigarette. I'd never seen anybody do anything quite so amazing. I took wooden matches from the metal matchbox holder by the stove and began to practice. Whenever I had free time I'd try to get one to light. Over and over I'd swish the match up the leg of my Levi's but never could I get a spark. Eventually my father caught me and saw what I was trying to do and why.

"Don't you ever let me see you trying such a thing again," Daddy stormed at me. "You are not an old broken down cowboy; you are a lady, and you're going to act like a lady. I will make sure you wear a skirt every day for the rest of your life if I ever see you trying that trick again." I didn't ever try that trick again, but I still didn't get what it meant to be a lady until the butchering incident. Then I was furious.

Butchering was one of the most important events of ranch life. We lived on the meat we raised on the ranch. My dad would decide which steer was to be butchered and have it brought into the corral. He sharpened all the knives, and we waited until dark so the flies wouldn't be too bad. Then we all headed to the slaughter pen, a fenced concrete slab, to butcher the steer. I never watched him die from one shot in the head and then bleed from a cut throat. My job was to shine a spotlight wherever the men were working. First the men lifted the young animal up onto a large hook where they gutted him and began quartering him. Afterward the men washed down the whole slaughter pen with soap and water, Daddy cleaned his knives and buckets, and the men brought the beef to the basement. We were always excited in anticipation of breakfast the next morning when we'd have fresh liver and sweetbreads, and then we'd have all the choice cuts of meat for weeks ahead.

One summer evening, when I was ten years old, I ran to get the big spotlight and started off with the men to the slaughter pen as it was again time to butcher. My father stopped me. "No, Sally, I'm not going to let you come with us to butcher anymore. This is not something ladies should be doing," he said flatly. I couldn't believe what I was hearing. Did he mean I could never help butcher anymore? Yes, that was exactly what he meant. I rushed back to the house and cried the whole time the men were butchering. Nothing my mother said consoled me. I screamed that I was never going to be a lady, no matter what my dad said.

I don't remember wishing I was a boy, even though it seemed Warner got to do many more fun things than I did, but I sure didn't want to be a lady either. Ladies obviously couldn't have any fun at all. I just wanted to be a ranch girl.

Years later at the University of Nevada I met the exact kind of ranch girl my father did not want me to be. She wore old beat-up boots and Levi's to class, cussed, struck matches on her pant leg, and smoked. It was not as impressive when she did it as when Ted Gardner did it. Still this girl from Austin, Nevada, intrigued me. Nobody was ever shocked to learn she was raised on a ranch. I wore skirts, sweater sets, a string of pearls, and pumps to class; and people could not believe I came from a ranch. "Sally, you don't have a masculine bone in your body," someone once said to me.

Well, Daddy wherever you are, you must be smiling. Your daughter seems to have turned out to be the very image of the lady you created for her from the first day she was born . . . but don't look too closely. Those people who know me well know . . . *images can be deceiving.*

My father's daughter - a lady?

28 My Friend Flicka

The wind was blowing the day my little palomino filly came to me; I didn't hear the truck pull up in the yard, and I was surprised to hear a knock on the back door. There she stood balancing on her long dangling legs. Johnny and Dean Adams were holding her by a rope halter. "We brought you a lonely little mustang," Dean said. Both boys laughed when I threw my arms around her neck, and she began to throw her head and paw the ground. "She's a mustang," Johnny said. "You're going to need to do some work before she'll make friends with you."

I was thirteen when the Adams boys, who lived on the ranch twelve miles north of ours, roped the mustang colt and decided I should have her. While "mustanging," they had killed her mother. Ranchers would round up mustangs back then and sell them to the glue factory because they competed with their cattle for the scrub brush and grass. Mustangs have no natural enemy, so they multiply quickly, and they keep cattle away from the scarce water holes. I fell in love with my little mustang immediately and named her Flicka.

We put her in our fenced front yard, then moved her to the orchard below the house. Ed said she needed milk, so that evening I brought her a bucket of fresh milk right from the spout of the separator in the milk cellar where Ed was separating the milk and cream. She turned and ran when I set the bucket down and didn't come near it until I left the field. Each day she allowed me to come closer to me. One morning as I approached her, she reared up on her hind legs and tried to stomp me. I backed up barely in time to escape her front hooves. After that she considered it great fun to chase me all over the pasture and try to stomp me. A smarter person would have given up on her, but I continued bringing her milk and running, all the while explaining that she'd need to behave or she'd be in the glue factory where all the other mustangs were that Johnny and Dean had caught. Mom took the milk to her once to see if Flicka would chase her; she was the perfect little lady and came right up to the bucket and drank.

"She thinks you're her mustang playmate," Ed told me.

I kept going inside the gate, talking softly to her, and moving closer to her. Eventually I got close enough to touch her and finally to put my arms around her neck. She stopped trying to tromp me into the ground and came to the bucket of milk while I was standing next to it. Each day she got tamer. I brought her to the front yard so I could spend more time with her. By the end of that summer, Flicka's behavior resembled a dog more than a horse. She would follow me around the ranch and lie down with me on the front lawn when we took an afternoon nap. I'd prop my head on her flank and sleep. It always irritated her when I'd go in the house and she'd have to stay outside. One day she learned to nuzzle the screen door open, and she followed me inside, right through the dining room and down into the kitchen where Mom was standing at the sink with her back to her. She jumped sky high when Flicka put her nose in Mom's back and began nudging her. After that we had to put a hook on the door to keep her outside.

At the end of the summer we moved back to town, and we put Flicka in the lower pasture. I lived for Friday when I could get back to my horse. I'd run to the field and whistle, and she'd come running. Every weekend we were inseparable.

The next summer I began to think about riding her. My dream had always been to have a really good barrel racing horse, so I could go to the rodeos in Lund, Eureka, Pioche, Alamo, McGill, and other small places in our part of the state. Even though my dad competed in roping events at the rodeos and won many trophies, he did not have the same vision for his daughter. I always had to ride hand-me-down horses. My cousin Guy's buckskin, Fidget, became my regular horse when she got older. Fidget was named for the trait he had of jumping and bucking whenever his hooves hit a bridge or when a bird flew up in front of him. When I finally inherited him, he could not buck as often or jump as high anymore. Still I landed on the ground a few times. I never knew when a bird would fly up while we were pushing cows across the flats. I'd practice barrel racing on Fidget by standing up bales of hay down in the meadow and circling them. Now I was sure I could break and train Flicka to become my dream horse.

Dad forbade me to get on her. He used the fact that horses should not be broken to ride until they were three years old, or they'd become swaybacked. That didn't wash with me because I knew I didn't weigh enough to sway

Flicka's back. He also told me it took a very experienced buckaroo to break a mustang, and many could never be broken. Whenever Dad left the ranch, I'd get my saddle out and try putting it on her.

She hated that saddle, so every time I'd put it on her, she'd make one high buck, and the saddle would fall off. I did not give up. Every chance I got I'd sneak out and try putting my saddle on Flicka's back. She acted like she couldn't wait for me to come play the saddle game with her. Finally, one day, I managed to get the saddle on, and the cinch almost fastened before she started to buck. When the saddle didn't come off with the first buck, she reared up, bucked, kicked her back legs, and pretty much went crazy. The cinch finally came loose, and the saddle flew into the air. It came crashing down right on Flicka's head. That was that. Now every time she even saw that saddle, she'd start to buck. I put the saddle away, but that didn't mean I gave up on riding my little filly.

I tied her really tight to the fence with a rope. Then I tied a scarf around her eyes and while I was sweet talking and loving her, I carefully slid onto her back. It took a few seconds before she realized I was actually on her, then she got very nervous and tried to sidestep with her hind legs and pull away from the fence. I lay down low over her neck and continued to rub and talk to her. Soon she realized she was safe, and she began enjoying the attention. After many hours of doing this, she eventually got used to me sitting on her back.

I spent every spare minute I could with Flicka that summer. We'd go through the lower meadow and out into the brush. I always stayed below the ranch, so my dad wouldn't see me. I remember thinking life could never be more perfect as I walked with her or sat on her in the hot summer sun. I dreamed that with Flicka I would become a champion barrel racer. I believed she trusted me enough that I could get a saddle on her someday soon, but I never got the chance to try again.

We moved back to town in September. Just one week later, when we came back to the ranch for the weekend, I jumped out of the car, ran to the pasture, and whistled. I knew immediately something was wrong. Ed was waiting by the fence. "She's done for, Sally," he said. "She got in the barbed wire, and she's real bad off." I followed him to the barn and began to cry when I saw her front leg. It was almost cut off. Ed doctored her leg for several weeks, but when the leg started to grow back together, it was three inches longer than her other legs; and it was very twisted. There was no chance she'd ever walk again. When a truck came to haul away other mustangs that had been rounded up for the glue factory, she was part of the load.

I always believed she had tried to get through the barbed wire fence because she missed me and wanted to find me. We had been together constantly that summer. For two long, wonderful years though, Flicka had been my best friend. And privately I now considered myself an experienced buckaroo because I had broken a mustang to ride.

Flicka in the front yard

Flicka and Sally

Clair and Diamond with one of their many roping trophies

29 *A Bed Story*

My father always brought me to the ranch from Ely the week before school was out in the spring to work on the house and yards. I loved getting out of school a week early each year even though I worked hard for one solid week. Daddy wanted everything clean for when the family moved back for the summer. The first thing I always did was to get the beds out of the storeroom. I'd drag the mattresses into the yard and hang all the bedding and my flannel pajamas on the lines to air out. I'd drag the army cots out and hose the bugs and spider webs off them then my dad helped me move the cots onto the lawn at the North side of the house where Warner and I usually started sleeping every summer. I'd put a box between our cots where I set a large battery, a small olive green plastic radio, and a flashlight. I had many jobs to do that week to get the place ready for the family, but getting my bed ready was one of the most important ones.

I needed to spread out the huge canvas tarp on the lawn. Then I would place the mattress on the tarp and lay the flannel sheet folded longways on top of the mattress. Next I would put wool blankets over the sheet one at a time and fold them under the mattress on both sides. Finally I'd bring the tarp in on both sides and up from the bottom leaving a long flap at the top to cover my head in case it rained. If I did a good job, I'd not have to redo my bedroll for the entire summer.

Warner and I would move our cots all over the ranch. Behind the storeroom, under the granary, up in the tree house my dad built when he was a boy, under the mulberry trees. I took off my boots every night and put them on the ground, then I'd climb into my bedroll with my clothes on. I could take all my clothes off under the covers, roll them in a ball and put them under my pillow, and then put my pajamas on. Being able to dress and undress under the covers is one of many exceptional skills I acquired while living on the ranch.

We'd slept on the lawn for several weeks one summer when I decided I was ready for a move. I loved to listen to the coyotes each night as I was going to sleep. I suggested that we should move our cots to what we still called the orchard below the house even though every fruit tree had been burned out long before. We'd be closer to the field and the coyotes. Warner was not enthralled with coyotes at all, and he refused to move to the orchard. In fact, that summer he was not particularly enthralled with me either, so he decided to move his bed on top of the machine shed. After he helped move me to the orchard, I helped him lift his cot up a long wooden ladder onto the slanting tin roof of the machine shed. We found an old piece of carpet to put his bed on so it would not slide off. Then he pulled the ladder up so nobody (namely me) could climb up and bother him. He decided he should have the flashlight.

I placed the box next to my bed then set my radio and battery on it. That night I headed off to bed with a box of matches to light my way, striking one every few steps. I pulled my boots off and put them on the ground then crawled into bed. Soon my wish came true. The coyotes began to howl, and they sounded so much closer than when I was up by the house. They sounded closer than they did five minutes ago. I stopped breathing and listened. They were coming closer every time they howled. I thought about lighting a match because it was very dark. Much darker than it had ever been up at the house. I was paralyzed with fear as I crawled deeper and deeper into my sleeping bag. The next thing I knew, it was quiet. I waited with my heart pounding. Then I scooted up to the top of my bed and slowly peered out realizing morning had come, and nothing had eaten me.

"So how was the new bedroom?" my mother asked when I came in the house to help with breakfast.

"Oh, just the best. It was super. I've always wanted to be able to hear coyotes that well," I answered. "But I've found an even more perfect place to put my bed. Warner, will you help me move it sometime this morning?"

We did move my bed one more time. It was not easy getting it situated on both sides of the creek. I had measured so I knew the huge hole in the big tree where I put the head of my bed was just the right size for my radio and battery and my box of matches along with a tin cup in case I got thirsty. The foot of my bed was on the opposite bank. This turned out to be the perfect place. The creek I loved so much flowed right under my bed, so I had cool, clear water to drink, watercress to eat, and running water to put me to sleep. We later set up another army cot and bedroll beside my bed in case a friend came to stay, and it was a place to put my boots. I kept my bed in that spot for all the rest of my summers on the ranch until I was twenty years old. I think Warner was jealous of my perfect spot, but he kept his bed on the roof of the machine shed until he got married.

Warner slept on top of machine shed

30 *A Day Off*

Nothing is really work unless you would rather be doing something else.

One day in my fourteenth summer, my mother announced that she wanted to start paying me $1.50 a day and giving me time off. "You will get one day a week off." She told me, "You should have some time and money of your own." How could I argue? I would now get paid for the work I had been doing for nothing and have a day off besides.

The next day I decided to take my day off. I got up as usual and began setting plates on the table for breakfast, but Mom insisted that I was not to do anything on my day off, so I stood and watched her finish setting the table and pull the rope outside the back door to ring the dinner bell. The hired men came in to eat a breakfast of pancakes, eggs, bacon, and strong coffee. My job was always to cook the pancakes, but I sat at the table while Mom fried bacon and eggs and then began cooking pancakes. I was a little upset that she did such a good job. Wasn't I the best pancake cook on the ranch? Maybe not the smartest.

I once backed up against the gas burner while I was waiting for a batch of pancakes to cook and caught my shirt on fire. Flames climbed up my back, and I froze. Six men sat at the table just ten feet from me, and I guess I decided to burn up rather than rip my shirt off in front of them. Finally, when I began to feel the heat against my skin, I turned and tried to get into the room behind the kitchen, but the door was stuck. Just as my dad jumped up to grab my shirt, the door opened, and I escaped into the bedroom. There were a few small burns on my back, but Dad brought me another shirt and breakfast continued.

That day instead of clearing the table and starting the dishes, I began making myself a peanut butter and jelly sandwich. I placed it on a dish towel with a can of Vienna sausage and a can opener, tied the towel up in

171

a knot, and headed to the saddle house. I had decided to take Fidget for a long ride.

The sun warmed my face as I started across the bench above the ranch and headed into the foothills where the terrain began to change from scrub and sage brush to small pine trees. Finally I decided I was hungry, so I got off my horse, took my lunch and a canteen of water out of my saddle bag, and sat down under a tree by Margaret Lillian, my dog, who had decided to come along. When I looked at my watch, I saw that it was only 9:30. I had been gone just two hours. I thought about my mother and realized she had probably already washed the dishes and the huge metal bowl and the twenty-seven other pieces of the cream separator and had lugged them all back to the milk cellar by herself. Now she'd probably be kneading the bread to put into loaves. She would have saved out some dough, and there would be scones for lunch. My mouth watered to think of the fried bread with butter and syrup. I climbed back on Fidget and continued climbing the mountain. *If I started back now*, I thought, *I could be back home in time to help Mom with the lunch dishes. No*, I thought, *this is my day off.* I continued climbing. Several more minutes passed, and then I turned my horse around, and the three of us headed back home.

"Why are you back?" Mom asked. "This is your day off."

"Well," I said as I filled the sink with soapy water, "maybe I'll start with half a day off and work up to a whole day." Mother smiled and then she went into her bedroom and lay down to rest her legs. *If I had not come back, she could not have taken that few minutes off*, I thought.

A week went by, and it was time again for my next day off. I decided to hang around the ranch that day. There were no books, but I still had a *Seventeen* magazine which I took with me down to the big wooden bridge. I had read it once, but there was a fiction story that I could read again. It was "to be continued" about a young girl who was quite fat but a young man was showing some interest in her. For the rest of the summer I asked anybody who went to town to look for the next issue of *Seventeen* magazine. I could not wait to read the rest of that story. As I sat on the creek bank leaning against the bridge, I noticed the garden. The hoe was laying in the middle of a row where Ed had obviously stopped weeding. *Here is what I can do*, I thought. *I can do something to help Ed.* By the time I hoed to the top of the row, I realized that this was not what I wanted to do with my day off.

Had anybody thought to cut some meat for Mom before they left today? I thought. If not it would be impossible for her to lift the side of beef off the hook in the basement. Even if she did get it down and did get steaks or a roast cut off, she could not get it hung back up. It took both of us to go to the basement where the meat stayed cool for several weeks after it was butchered, lay it on the bench, and cut off what we needed for the day. I considered going back to the house. *No,* I thought, *this is my day off.* I decided to walk down to the field and see if Ed needed help with the irrigating.

Margaret Lillian and I took our time walking along the dirt road to the reservoir. Suddenly Margaret froze, and she began a deep, low growl. Every hair on her back stood up, and I knew she had seen something out of the ordinary. What she saw turned out to be the most amazing thing I had ever seen and have ever seen in my lifetime since. There in the road in front of us was a blow snake that had sucked up the front half of a huge jackrabbit. I could hear the faint cry of the rabbit even though its head was inside the snake. Its back legs were wildly kicking. As the snake continued to suck in the rabbit, its body expanded to accommodate the animal. I stood without moving, barely breathing, as I watched the rabbit slowly disappear in front of my eyes. Margaret continued to growl, but she did not go closer. Even she seemed to understand the wonder of this scene. In about ten minutes the rabbit was gone and the large, bloated snake continued to lay in the road. I didn't think it would be moving for a long time, so after watching it for quite a while, Margaret and I ran all the way back to the house to get Mom. We came back down in the truck, but the snake had moved, and it was nowhere to be found. Still I had seen it, and the whole incident is as clear today as it was that morning over sixty years ago. I didn't stop talking about it for the whole summer.

Mom needed me every day that next week because she decided we should paint the kitchen. The next week my dad decided I was old enough to start running the tractor. I loved going to the field every morning to rake hay while Warner mowed and Dad baled.

Not an experienced tractor driver, I would get too close to the ditch bank, and the tractor would drop off into the ditch. I had to walk and wave until I got Warner's attention in the next field so he could come pull me out. The first time we had to take his tractor clear back to the house to get a chain, and Warner was not happy. The second time he was really not happy. So when I got to the row of cut hay beside the ditch bank the third time, I decided to get off the tractor and move the entire windrow away from the ditch. The windrow was damp and heavy, but I pushed it one turn away from the ditch bank for the entire length of the field. When I got to the end of the field, I could not stand up. I had pulled or slipped something in my back. The pain was so awful that I had to crawl across the field this time to get Warner's attention. Dad drove me to Ely to a chiropractor that afternoon. That was my only trip to town that summer.

After the hay was mowed, raked, and baled, Warner and I hauled the bales back to the hay yard to stack. We had a baled hay loader hooked on the right front of the hay wagon. My job was to drive the tractor so the slide on the hay loader lined up perfectly with the bale, and it would go up a belt and land on the hay wagon where Warner would stack it. The bales were not always laying straight in the field, so this was not easy to do. I'd have to get off the tractor and move the bale around to the front of the loader if I missed. Each bale weighed close to eighty pounds. My back hurt most of the summer, but I was able to stand upright, so I don't remember complaining.

Mother continued to pay me $1.50 per day because I was able to do the breakfast dishes and get the cream separator washed while the men were gassing up the tractors and working on equipment in the mornings. I could do the lunch dishes when everyone was lying down for a thirty-minute rest before returning to the field. We came back from the field at 5:00 p.m., so I could help Mom get supper on and do the dishes.

A day off was never discussed again, and that was okay with me. I learned early on that if I wanted to be with my mother or get any attention from my father, I had to work along beside them. I learned to love work.

Sally on her 'day off'

31 The Bomb

"It's got to be because of the bomb."

"The bomb caused it."

Out on our ranch in the early 1950s, the bomb jokingly got blamed for everything from the drought to the hay baler breaking down. "The bomb" we were referring to was the aboveground atomic bomb testing which began in 1951 just eighty miles (as the crow flies) from our ranch.

For a young teenage girl living on an isolated cattle ranch in eastern Nevada, the whole thing was very exciting. There had been times when my greatest pleasure had been seeing dust from a car twelve miles away, hoping that it might stop at the ranch. Now trucks were pulling into the yard on a regular basis, and many times good-looking young men in flannel shirts and straw cowboy hats got out to visit with us. The Atomic Energy Commission (AEC) were everywhere those summers. They usually showed up right after a bomb had been dropped. They'd test the water and soil in the area. Everyone got their drinks of water from the cold water in the creek by our back door. We drank from a tin cup hanging on a stump next to the cement bridge. Everyone who stopped at the ranch or lived on the ranch drank from that tin cup. I remember the AEC men dipping that cup into the creek and then saying that was the best water they'd ever tasted.

We'd wear badges they gave us which measured the amount of radiation we were receiving. Each month my dad collected the badges from our family, Ed Rowlie, and all the other hired men at Sunnyside. He put them in a special envelope and mailed them to the AEC according to their instructions. We never got the results of the badges and have often wondered what ever happened to them.

Even more exciting, we would hear by way of our big battery operated RCA radio in the corner of the living room that a bomb would be set off early on a certain morning. We could get KSL from Salt Lake City after dark and as the testing got in full swing, the AEC began announcing the times of the tests. My dad would set the alarm clock, wake us up, and make a pot of coffee. We would each carry a chair from the back step to the open yard below the house. Then we'd get ourselves seated comfortably and proceed to wait for the big event as though it were a fireworks display on the Fourth of July. Presently, we would see an enormous flash so bright that we needed to look away for a few seconds. Next the entire southwest sky would light up, and the smoke and dust rose slowly into a perfect column which then formed into a huge mushroom cloud. As we watched, it would very slowly begin to dissipate. The sight, just at daybreak, was spectacular. We never missed a bomb if we could help it.

Some of the ranchers during those years questioned the threat of the nuclear fallout from the bombs. The men from the AEC who came around were pleasant and willing to answer our questions.

"You are in a very real sense active participants in the nation's atomic test program. These tests are contributing greatly to building the defenses of our own country and the free world."

At times, we were told, some of us had been exposed to potential risk from flash, blast, or fallout; but we accepted this risk without fuss, alarm, or panic. Our cooperation had helped achieve an unusual safety record. Nevada's senator, Howard Cannon, said that there were so few people living downwind of the bombing that it made the Nevada test site a perfect place to drop the bombs. They were trying to keep the fallout to the absolute minimum, but the dangers that might occur from the fallout involve a small sacrifice when compared to the infinitely greater evil of the use of nuclear bombs in war.

The AEC made very sure that they would never drop a bomb when the winds were blowing south toward Las Vegas. When the wind would blow north and east so the fallout would pass over sparsely populated areas, isolated ranches like ours, the conditions were perfect. Often as we moved our cattle from the winter range south of the ranch to the summer range in the mountains to the north, fallout dust from an atomic test would fill the sky and settle on the ground around us.

My cousins' ranch at Hiko, seventy miles south of Sunnyside, was near the small town of Alamo. Alamo was just forty miles from Jackass Flat where the bombs were detonated. Each time a bomb was about to be dropped, the government sent military buses to the Pahranagat Valley to evacuate the people in case the wind turned.

In July 1962, my cousin Keith was on his tractor, haying when he felt what he first thought were bug bites up both his arms. Then his face began to burn, and he looked up to see radiation fallout settling over his fields. Remembering the buses he'd seen in the valley during previous tests, he jumped off his tractor and drove his truck to Alamo where he could be evacuated. But when he got there, no bus could be seen anywhere. Apparently, that day, when the bus drivers realized the wind had turned and the fallout was drifting directly over them, they took off without waiting for any people to board the buses. He did watch men from the AEC hose radiation off the cars before they were allowed to leave either end of the valley though. That bomb was known as Dirty Harry, and it was so lethal that anyone who lived in any of five Nevada counties or parts of Utah during that month in 1962, who got cancer, became eligible for a compensation payment from the government.

My Aunt Ouida remembered a time when she had to stop the school bus she was driving to Alamo and wait for a dense radiation cloud to pass over so she could continue delivering the children to their homes. These children had been unable to go outside for recess that morning due to the thick fallout from the bomb.

As it turned out, we had good reason to blame the bomb for some things. My Hiko cousins, Kent and Kathryn, developed cancer. Kent died at age thirty-nine leaving five children. His sister, Kathryn, developed a slower growing type of cancer twenty years later. She is still alive, but after all these years she is about to start one more experimental drug to control the growth of tumors in her lungs. The government "compensated" them. Fifty thousand dollars for Kent's family, and $50,000 to Kathryn. This was an amount established in a bill by Congress when the government took responsibility for the leukemia, birth defects, sterility, miscarriages, and cancer of the "downwind" people. A huge percentage of people in that small community have gotten cancer. Interestingly, Keith, who is now almost eighty, is not one of them.

In 2003, fifty years after we sat in our backyard watching mushroom clouds billow into the sky, I was diagnosed with breast cancer. The government must have thought the bomb was to blame because after filing a claim, I received a $50,000 check from the Radiation Exposure Compensation Program, U. S. Department of Justice. Many more kinds of cancers have been added to the compensation program now and all the "downwinder" settlements are $50,000.

The atomic bomb testing caused great grief and anguish to many families who lived in some parts of Nevada, Utah, and Arizona between 1951 and 1958 or in July of 1962. We "downwinders" are not at all convinced it was for the good of the world as our government had assured us it was.

Watching atomic bomb go off circa 1952

32 *Princess Pretty Feet*

I ordered a turquoise squaw dress from my dad's western clothing catalog when I was about sixteen. Mom helped me with the order after getting Daddy's permission. I was sure he would give us permission because he always wanted me to act and dress like a lady. Instead I wore my "stand alone" Levi's which my mother would try to snatch from my room and wash while I was asleep, but I would jump out of bed and grab them out of her hands. I'd wear the same pair of Levi's all summer, but it would be July before they started feeling really comfortable, and that was only if they had never been washed. I'd put my Levi's in my bedroll at the end of the summer, so I could wear them when we moved back to the ranch in the spring. Somehow they'd disappear during the winter, and I'd have to start over with a fresh pair. I'd also wear Warner's old shirts and greasy cowboy hats that he didn't want anymore.

My dad was pleased with my new dress. He always ordered the best the western catalogs had to offer for himself. His dress shirts had western style yokes and mother-of-pearl snaps up the front. He'd lay his best Stetson hat on the dining room table and spend all evening powdering it with white chalk. When every inch was bright white, he'd brush it with a special brush then carefully wrap it in tissue paper and store it in a hat box in his closet. He specially ordered his boots after sending a mold of his feet to a company in Arizona because his feet always hurt. He loved nice clothes and wanted his daughter to look at least "presentable" if not respectable. The squaw dress was just the thing for me.

Mom thought I could wear the dress when I went to church while visiting with Kathryn at Hiko. I even talked them into ordering me a beautiful silver Concho belt and some white rawhide moccasins to wear with my dress because my boots were not fit to wear off the ranch. The story about my friend Ann who came to stay on the ranch with me several times will explain my boots. She asked for cowboy boots like Sally's for Christmas one year, but when she opened the large box under the Christmas tree, she began to cry. "These boots don't look like Sally's," she said. "I want them to be all scuffed up and have manure on them." She remembers her dad trying to scuff them up at little, but the manure thing was out of the question.

My squaw dress was made of a heavy crinkled cotton. The top had a zipper in the back, a mandarin collar, and dark turquoise, red, gold and silver rickrack across the bodice. The skirt had a waistband with two wide ruffles. It was fuller at the bottom, so I loved to turn around and around so the skirt would flare out in front of me. I couldn't wait to go to Hiko where I could really wear my dress—not just put it on for a little while in the afternoons at the ranch. The people in Alamo probably thought I'd come off an Indian reservation when I showed up for church in my new garb. I thought I looked absolutely gorgeous.

I wore it in Ely when we had costume day at school or when I was in a skit. I made a headband out of black cloth, rickrack, and sequins and sewed little casings for beautiful bird feathers I found on the ranch. I looked like a very blonde Indian princess. I soon got the name Princess Pretty Feet because I went barefoot and bragged about my beautiful feet quite often. "My toes are even and straight—no toe too long or too short. When the light catches my feet at just the right angle," I'd say, "you can see just how perfectly formed they are."

When I went off to college at Utah State, I packed my dress, moccasins, and headdress in the trunk of Warner's car along with my hoopskirt and yards of dirndl petticoats. I remember wearing it only once to a sorority costume party.

Several years ago I gave my squaw dress to the Goodwill because I could no longer zip the back zipper. Just as we need to let go of periods of time in our past, clothes are part of those times, so we need to let them go too. Sadly, not only is my squaw dress gone, but so are my beautiful feet. It is painful for me to walk now because I have arthritis in both feet. They are deformed and swollen. I'm not eager to show them to anyone.

How does the saying go? *"After the pride cometh the fall."*

33 *My Secret Love*

Two longs, two shorts, and a long. That was Adams' ring! I was standing right next to the phone on the wall above the desk, so I lifted the receiver and instantly knew it was Johnny's voice. I held my breath when I heard him tell Clay Hendrix that he would be coming down that afternoon to pick up a calf. This meant that Johnny Adams would be driving by my ranch but would not be stopping. I knew I had to try to see him.

From the time a dust appeared at the cedars just this side of Adams' Ranch, it took a car about thirty minutes to get to the ranch, so I washed my face and changed my blouse and watched for a dust. The ranch had reluctantly given Mom a few rare minutes to curl up on the living room couch and read. If she noticed my clean blouse, she didn't say anything.

I waited a few minutes longer before I started up to the road. His truck got closer, and the dust got higher. Then the question occurred to me: what possible reason could I give for being up on the road in the middle of the afternoon? I darted into the brush just as the old gray International truck went plowing by in such a dust that I wasn't even able to see the driver. He was gone. I sat by the road in my dusty, clean blouse and stared sadly at the disappearing dust. He would be coming back by later, but I knew I wouldn't see him then either, for there wouldn't be time to watch for him. Late that night as I lay on my cot over the creek, I heard his truck go by heading north.

I'd been in love with Johnny Adams since eighth grade when his family had bought the Riordan ranch, twelve miles north of Sunnyside. I thought about him during the days as I was doing my work, and I dreamed about him at night. I figured as long as thinking and dreaming about him didn't interfere with my work, it was okay. The best relationships I've had with men have been in my dreams.

Sometimes I would talk Mom into letting us stop at Adams' Ranch on

Friday nights on our way back to Sunnyside from Ely. Usually Johnny was not home, but just being in the big old house where he lived and visiting with his mother gave me joy. One afternoon I even drove up to see Erma, Johnny's mom, and helped her do her ironing. She showed me how to iron western shirts with rivets on them, and I was sure at least one of them must have been Johnny's. She talked about her three boys: Vernile, Johnny, and Dean. I thought maybe she wished one of them would marry me.

One afternoon Johnny came to the ranch looking for my dad. It was a rare afternoon when I had bathed, washed my hair, and put on a clean blouse. I wasn't even nervous as I walked with him to find Daddy. Talking to him seemed easy. I took him to the pasture to see my little buckskin mustang, Flicka, that Johnny and his brothers had brought me after her mother had been killed. I explained how I could put a halter on her now and could lead her around the corral, but at first, when I brought her buckets of milk, she'd rare up and try to stomp me and the bucket. I was even more crazy about Johnny after that day, and I believed he now saw me differently too. I dared think that someday we'd be together.

The Adams boys went to school in Lund while my family had moved to Ely for school, so I only saw Johnny a few times each summer. My father thought the boys didn't work hard enough because they often took days off, and they went to church on Sundays in Lund—even during haying season.

Their parents, Myron and Erma, drove to Sunnyside a few times on Saturday evenings to visit with Mom and Daddy. They'd bring Kate, who was Bonnie's age, but the boys never came. Since they took Sunday off at their ranch, Myron and Erma would stay and visit for a while. One night my dad, who was very tired and knew he'd be up at five o'clock the next morning, said, "Well, Mom, why don't we go to bed, so these nice people can go home?" My mother was mortified. Myron had a huge belly hanging over his Levi's, and he walked slow and talked very slow—too slow for my dad. One Saturday evening, he asked Myron why he talked so darn slow.

"W e l l, i f y o u c a n ' t t h i n k f a s t, t a l k s l o w," was his response. Mom and Daddy were really very good friends with Myron and Erma.

Dean Adams was one month younger than me, but he was a year behind me in school. We became good friends. He remembers a time when he, Warner, and I saw a wild steer out on the range while we were in Daddy's Ford truck. I told them I would ride it if they could catch it. We raced across the alkali flat in that truck with a lasso rope for an hour or so before we gave up trying to catch him. Dean even went to my high school graduation party in Ely with Kathryn, Kent, and me.

Dean made a comment later on in our lives that made me think he probably knew me better than my own family. In fact, all the people who lived on the neighbor ranches probably knew me better than my own family. We had all gone to Clay Hendrix's funeral in Fallon in the 1970s. After the funeral, Finley Hendrix said to me, "So, Sally, are you living on a ranch somewhere?"

"No," I said, "I live in a small house near the prison in Carson City."

"I can't imagine you living in a city," he said.

"I can't imagine Sally even living in a house," Dean added.

I also got to know Johnny's older brother, Vernile, the summer after my high school graduation in 1956. He came to work for my dad, and I went to Ely to a movie with him once or twice mostly because I thought we might stop at Adams' Ranch and I would see Johnny. Vernile did want to marry me. And once, I was positive Johnny wanted to marry me too.

I did get to see Johnny quite a bit that summer, even though he was dating a girl from Lund. I started going up to Adams' Ranch on Saturday nights with Vernile. I'd run the calf roping while the three boys practiced rodeoing. I'd bring the flag down and drop the rope barrier as the calf came out of the chute. Then I would time the roper to see how long it took to rope and tie the calf. They dared me, so once I even rode one of the calves (but not for long). That was the best summer of my life. For one thing I was with Johnny, and for another I loved being with the boys. Even after a year of college at Utah State University in Logan, Utah, I still had a serious crush on Johnny Adams.

*Johnny Adams' graduation picture from Lund High School
(second from right)*

34 Whipple Cave

In about 1904, Grandpa, his brother Charles, and Uncle Vern discovered Whipple Cave while moving cattle to the summer range in Cave Valley. They were chasing a wild calf along the foothills six miles northeast of Sunnyside in the South Egan Mountain Range when it fell into a huge sink hole in the mountain. Peering in they saw what looked like a large cave leading deep into the mountain.

They got several men from Lund and returned with long lengths of rope, lanterns, and torches and let themselves into the forty feet diameter hole. The first drop was sixty-five feet to a small ledge and then another six feet to the floor of the cave which looked flat from the top. It was more like a steep forty-five-degree angle hill. As they began walking almost straight down into the black void, they realized they were in a magnificent cave with spectacular formations, huge caverns, popcorn, crystals growing up walls, cascading pools of water, and a seventy-foot column which they later learned is the largest stalagmite in North America. The largest chamber was one-half mile long covered with a roof one hundred feet high. They got at least three hundred feet deep. This turned out to be greater in size than any known cave west of the Rocky Mountains.

From then on Whipple Cave became a major form of recreation for the people of Lund and our family. They would drive to the base of the mountain and make the short hike to the entrance. A wooden ladder was built which rotted in the 1920s and was replaced with a metal chain ladder with round spacers at each rung. Daddy's family lowered tables and benches into the cave and spent weekends camping and exploring when he was growing up. They used carbide and kerosene lamps. Elwood remembers the many Easters spent in the cave. The Whipple siblings met with spouses and children at the cave where dyed eggs were hidden in the brush above the cave. They picnicked inside the cave.

Guy and Elwood took Warner and me into the cave whenever they had free time and Daddy was not around. Guy was always sure there was a larger room he would discover. He'd hold me by my skinny little legs when I was five or six years old and shove me facedown through narrow flat crevices. I remember my nose being squeezed as my face got pushed through the very narrow moist crevices. I'd hold a flashlight over my head and shine it around and report to Guy. I don't remember what I saw, but I know we never found a larger room. My dad would have killed Guy if he'd known what he was doing. Elwood tells me I was never afraid to do anything.

Even after Guy and Elwood stopped working every summer on the ranch, Warner and I would get the old ladder and go to the cave. We did this when we were sure our dad was not around. Once Warner and I and a couple of friends found a scorpion when we got to the bottom, so we pushed it into a tomato soup can. It was so long its stinger curled back over its body to its head. Fortunately, the cold dampness in the cave caused it to be lethargic. Later when Mom helped us put it in a coffee can with a lid at the ranch, it came to life. I don't remember how long we kept it, but I do remember Mom telling us we'd better not tell Daddy where we found it.

Exploring Whipple Cave became the highlight of our family reunions at Sunnyside and later at Hiko. We'd all get up to the cave in the back of trucks, hike the short distance, take turns tying a rope around our waists, and climb down on the chain ladder. Most of us had mag lights around our heads. The last time we all went in, the climbers varied in age from three years old to age sixty-seven. That day it began to rain, and someone decided to build a fire at the bottom. We were nearly asphyxiated from the smoke before we all got out. Many of my girl cousins had never been inside the cave, and they were sobbing by the time they got to the bottom on the old ladder. One metal rung was broken which meant we had to feel our way to the next rung. We also needed to walk across the ledge and catch the six-foot metal ladder to get to the bottom. Some said they could never go back up that ladder, and it took some persuading to get them out. When it was my turn to go back up, I heard Keith, who was managing the rope ladder from the top, say, "Don't worry about this one; it's Sally." He started shaking the ladder. Fortunately, since I had practically grown up in that cave, I hung on tight and got to the top without appearing to even be scared. I did get scared sometimes around my older boy cousins, but I never let them know.

Grandpa thought he had sold Whipple Cave twice—once to Gary Cooper who was going to make it into an underground gambling casino. The deal fell through when making a walk-in entrance, lighting the cave, and transporting people to it proved to be much too expensive. For years we kept Whipple Cave in our family as a mining claim, and some of us would meet to "do improvements" once a year so our claim could stay current. That would mean raking around a few sage brush, moving a few rocks, and having yet another picnic at the top of the cave. Our family sold it to the state twenty or more years ago, but we still consider it our cave. Because it is in an isolated part of the state and is hard to find, it remains much the same as it was when Grandpa discovered it over one hundred years ago. It is a prime cave for professional spelunkers because of its size and the amazing stalagmite.

Guy died of cancer many years ago. Warner and Elwood (who is in his eighties now) and I have decided we'll let the younger generation go into the cave during our family reunions from now on. We think we've explored every corner of it. I can, without question, say I've seen places in Whipple Cave that nobody else in the world has seen—thanks to my cousin Guy.

Spectacular popcorn formations inside Whipple Cave

Family spending a day at Whipple Cave during a reunion

40 ft. wide hole leading to magnificent cave

Sally climbing into Whipple Cave

Largest stalagmite in North America found in Whipple Cave

35   *A Not So Famous Reporter*

When I was about ten years old, I saw a picture of a reporter wearing a trench coat in the *Ely Daily Times* newspaper delivered by the mail truck twice a week. Mail and newspapers came to us in a leather mail bag the mail driver hung on our front gate. The caption under the picture read "Many Famous Reporters Go Abroad." I didn't know where abroad was, but it was someplace I hoped to go so I could write stories and become a famous reporter.

I decided to get a headstart on my career by publishing my own newspaper. That summer, wearing my dad's raincoat and carrying a notebook and pencil, I walked around the ranch collecting stories. When I had enough news for a full page, I'd sit at Daddy's desk in the dining room with a ruler, paper, and several pieces of carbon paper and "publish" my stories. If I pushed really hard with the pen, I could make three copies at a time. I'd draw a horizontal line near the top of the page and print SUNNYSIDE TIMES in large capital letters above it. Then I'd draw about three vertical lines from that line to the bottom of the page where I'd write in my stories. I'd have to rewrite the newspaper one more time using more carbon paper and paper because three of my aunts, Ed, and my mother agreed to subscribe to my newspaper. Since they were each giving me a dime, I figured they should all have a readable copy.

I never seemed to run out of exciting stories that summer. Ed was always finding new litters of kittens in the barn. I would describe each kitten in detail and even give the exact day they opened their eyes. Once a young tomcat killed all the kittens in a new litter. That was, of course, my headline story. A few times that summer, my mother, Bonnie or I would have to bottle-feed a leppy, newborn lamb, when a ewe would die or refuse to feed her baby.

My uncle Al got caught in a cloud burst coming through the gap one afternoon. When he didn't get to the ranch by the next day, Daddy drove out there and pulled his truck out of a deep wash where he'd been stuck for almost twelve hours.

One of the ranch dogs, Kanella, went into seizures after eating poison set out for coyotes. Daddy poured baking soda down her throat but could not save her.

A female coyote was sneaking into the chicken coop at night and taking one hen at a time back to her den for her pups. My dad backed his truck downwind of the chicken coop then put his sleeping bag onto a piece of plywood he laid across the rack of the truck. He waited several hours with a rifle next to his pillow. Finally he heard a small, faint, little squawk and looked up just as the coyote was coming out of the coop with a hen in her mouth. My father shot her instantly with one bullet. We knew her pups would probably die without a mother or food, but she was taking the sources of our eggs, and she had to be stopped.

I had trouble writing the story about my dog Ginger who began sucking eggs. We did everything we could to keep her from digging or clawing through the henhouse to get our eggs. Finally she had to be shot. I howled for days.

There was always great excitement when the eggs under my mother's setting hens would hatch. I checked on them every time I walked by the setting coups. When they hatched, I counted the baby chicks and gave details of their progress, writing the exact date when we moved them from the small coops to the large pen.

A carnival came to Ely early that summer. Kids could win baby ducks by throwing coins in a dish. Before the summer was over, many of them ended up at Sunnyside because these ducklings were adorable when they were babies, but when they got older they could get mean, they were messy and they obviously needed water to swim in. Our beautiful creek was the perfect place for them to glide along the water and clean out the watercress. I had a news-breaking story when my mother came back from a trip to Ely with a box full of baby ducks. Every summer after that a few more "carnival" ducks came to live with us.

Lucky for me, that summer happened to be the one we always remembered as "the summer of the skunks." I always had a skunk story for my paper. What we actually had were civet cats. They were smaller than skunks and deadlier because they did not need to be threatened to throw off their odor. They were everywhere that summer. We found shooting them didn't work because they'd begin to stink immediately when they were hit and continued to smell even after they had died. I have no idea how we learned the technique that worked in getting rid of all those little creatures that summer. Every time someone smelled, then spotted one, we'd start a car or truck up, stick the garden hose in the exhaust, and ease the other end as close to the skunk as we could get. Every time, the skunk would come over to the end of the hose and sniff, turn and leave, come back and sniff. By the third sniff it would pass out. This never failed. One of us would then get a bucket of water to drown him in and take him to the orchard where he'd be buried with the rest of his kind. The method was painless and effective. One morning a dog made connections with one of our stinky cats and had to be washed down with cans of tomato juice. Each skunk incident warranted a headline story in the SUNNYSIDE TIMES.

My aunts faithfully mailed me a dime each time they received one of my newspapers. That summer, I published, printed, and distributed about eight papers which cost three cents each to mail, so I figure I made a whopping $3.75. With that kind of success under my belt, I moved ahead with my career goal and majored in journalism at all the many universities I attended after high school. However, it was not in the cards that I should become a famous reporter. I changed my major and didn't ever get a degree in journalism. I did find out where abroad is though, and I have even been there, but now I'd rather become a published author than a famous journalist. I have continued to write journals, letters, and stories all my life.

Carnival ducks

36　Time Off on the Ranch

"Remember this puddle," Warner said as we were moving cattle back to the ranch from Blind Springs. When we got the cattle in the meadow and put our horses away, Warner and I loaded planks, shovels, hatchets, and even rope in the old truck. We then drove back to the puddle. I always knew what was in store for me when Warner pointed out a mud puddle.

"Over there!" I shouted, and he drove across the alkali flat right straight into the mud puddle where the truck sank clear to the axle. Now the fun began. First we got out our shovels and tried to fill in the mud puddle with dry dirt so the truck would come out. Our fun would be over if we got out on our first try. Next we got out our hatchets and chopped brush until we had large pieces stacked in front of both sunken tires. Then I jumped in the truck.

"Gun it!" Warner shouted to me as he got behind the truck and pushed. With tires spinning and mud flying, we were fortunately even more stuck. Now we would need to resort to using the planks which we placed in front of each tire in just the right places so Warner could drive the truck out of the mud puddle. We'd drive home several hours later with ourselves and the truck covered with mud. As usual Warner and I exchanged very few words. Even so, I liked being with Warner and by then there were fewer and fewer things that we did together.

Our time off at the ranch was usually minutes or sometimes hours if a job got completed ahead of schedule. While everyone rested for a few minutes after lunch, I'd hurry and wash the lunch dishes and drive up to the bench, a low, flat hill above the ranch, and listen to *One Man's Family* on the truck radio. It lasted for fifteen minutes and was a forerunner to today's soap operas. We couldn't get radio reception during the day at our house.

Water fights seemed to be a perfect time-out activity. They could start and end at any given time, and everyone got cooled off. We used everything from tin cups to coffee cans and buckets. Usually someone standing at the creek threw a cup of water through the kitchen window screen where one of the women was washing the dishes. She'd slam the window shut, fill a kettle, and heave water out the back door; or maybe somebody would get thrown in the creek. Either way, the fight was on. We'd run into the house quite often because it was off-limits. However, I remember seeing my mother sweeping water out of the kitchen and dining room back down into the ditch, so the house apparently wasn't always off-limits. The fight ended when my dad shouted, "Knock it off and get back to work."

Every evening after supper, Mom, Elva Braswell (our foreman's wife), and her daughter Carla Jean, Bonnie, and I would take a walk to the reservoir. This was something I always loved doing because the evenings were cool and the women were relaxed after the day's work was over. My father preferred to spend his evenings in the hammock on the front lawn. One evening Warner and I left in the truck right after supper to dig potatoes. We took Bonnie and Carla Jean with us. "I have an idea how we can scare Mom and Elva," Warner said to me. "I'll stand Bonnie on the seat and show her how to steer, and you get Carla on the floor and have her push the gas pedal just enough to move the truck slowly. When they see Bonnie driving, they'll panic."

Warner started the truck and explained to three-year-old Bonnie how to hold the steering wheel while standing on the seat. I had Carla, also three, on the floorboard pressing the gas pedal with her hands. Then both Warner and I jumped out and casually walked along each side of the truck. The timing was perfect because Elva and Mom came around the corner of the hay yard at just that moment and saw Bonnie driving the truck. They began frantically running down the road toward her, screaming and waving. The plan worked perfectly—for about two minutes. Then Carla pushed too hard on the gas pedal, and Bonnie panicked and steered the truck off the dirt road straight into a ditch where it crashed to a stop, but not before it had taken out a fence post and two rows of barbed wire. Bonnie was crying and bleeding from a cut lip. The following day, with "strong encouragement" from our father, Warner and I helped Ed replace the fence post by mixing cement in a wheelbarrow to dump in a posthole that we had both taken turns digging. That was not one of Warner's better ideas.

Another after supper activity was rabbit hunting. Dad did the shooting until Warner and I got older. Even then, I preferred driving the truck and running the spotlight. Warner and Dad would sit on the front fenders while Mom, Bonnie, and I sat in the cab.

The alfalfa fields were crawling with rabbits eating the hay we needed to bale and feed to the cattle in the winter. I drove cautiously across the field, then braked very slowly when a jackrabbit's eyes shone in the spotlight as I was slowly moving it back and forth in front of us. There were times in the fall when we poached (shot illegally) deer after dark. They consumed even more alfalfa than the rabbits, and alfalfa-fed venison has no wild taste so it tastes as good as beef. My dad made jerky out of at least one or two poached deer each summer.

Warner and my cousin Orvis and I will never forget the night during Thanksgiving break from college when we were poaching deer in the lower field. We noticed the lights from a car driving very slowly on the road above the ranch. "Oh Lord," Warner said, "that car is turning off the road toward the field. It's got to be the game warden!" We watched a few more minutes, and sure enough the lights were coming slowly toward us.

With several deer in the back of the truck and the truck lights turned off we took off out the back field. "You watch behind," Warner told me. "Orvis, help me see the road ahead." Just then we crashed. The truck dived straight into a very deep wash. After we assured each other that we were all right, we started digging our way out. We burned rubber off the tires and raced the motor for almost an hour, but we finally got out. We then drove slowly over a back road to the house. Thankfully, Daddy was asleep. We were trying to be very quiet while we told Mom what had happened. Suddenly there was a knock on the front door. We froze. We were sure it had to be the game warden. No, it was not. It was someone wanting to buy gas who didn't realize how far it was between gas stations.

After we were safely back to college, Daddy needed to use his truck. He discovered the axle was broken, and I can't remember what else. The truck was totaled. Bonnie wrote us a letter describing our father's reaction. Not pretty. By Christmas break, he had simmered down somewhat. We later found out that the lights coming toward us that night was from one of the Hendrixes on the next ranch. They were coming over to poach deer from our field.

I loved swimming at Hot Creek which was twelve miles from Sunnyside. The water was clear and warm and the tullies (a tall rodlike plant) had been cleared out in one area to make a pond. Water snakes swam through our legs and around our heads as we played and swam which didn't bother me, but a few of my friends from Ely refused to get in the water. Sometimes I'd ride Fidget over to Hot Creek by myself.

Daddy bought a motor scooter for Warner and me when we were teenagers. Warner piled up a huge mound of dirt in the hills above the ranch to make a jump. That gave us something else to do. It didn't do the scooter much good because we had a few bad crashes. We wore no helmets, so it didn't do us much good either. I took the scooter to Hot Creek swimming when I had an hour or two of free time in the afternoons.

Our family spent many summer evenings sitting on the back porch, watching what I thought was the most beautiful show on earth. As far as we could see across the valley, sheets of lightning would light up the whole sky. Other times the lightning would travel in flashes, or bolts would shoot in every direction and seem to hit the mountains far off in the distance. We counted the seconds after seeing the lightning to know when we'd hear the loud crash of thunder. A few times the storms were much closer, and lightning even hit our derrick once. Usually with the thunder and lightning, we got rain. Daddy was always happy then.

Whenever my aunts and uncles were visiting or Myron and Erma Adams came to spend a Saturday evening, Mom would cook the filling to put in our ice cream freezer then we'd take turns adding salt and ice and turning the handle on the freezer until the ice cream froze. I'd get to lick the paddle as it was pulled out of the freezer. We'd have homemade chocolate topping and freshly shelled walnuts for toppings.

Daddy didn't need a reason to make homemade honey candy. After dinner, he'd ask Mom to cook the syrup. She'd boil one cup cream, one cup honey, and one cup sugar to a hardball stage in a heavy-cast iron pan that was once my grandmother's pressure cooker, the pan I use to make candy and puddings today. Daddy would pour the candy into a platter until it cooled enough to pull. We all got a chunk to pull. I never got my piece pulled as perfectly as Daddy's. He pulled it until it was hard, long like a rope and white in color. Then, with scissors, he'd cut the rope into pieces and arrange them on a platter and place it on the dresser in the cold room—the bedroom off the kitchen. We were only allowed to eat one or two pieces each day. Once we were making popcorn balls, but Mom let the candy turn to sugar. She poured it over popped corn in a large bowl, and from then on sugarcoated popcorn was everybody's favorite.

I remember standing by my mother at the kitchen sink when I was eight or nine complaining that I was bored. She suggested things I could do, but what I really wanted was a friend. Then I started a club. I draped a sheet over a rope tied between two trees in the front yard to make my clubhouse. I brought all my dolls into the meeting. I, of course, was the president. I wrote minutes, so I must have also been the secretary.

When I got older, a friend from Lund would come to stay for a few days. Mirriam Thompson would ride the mail truck from Lund on Tuesdays and go back home when the truck came again on Fridays. She became the secretary of my club.

Girls from Ely would sometimes come to the ranch with me on a weekend or in the summers. Betty Isaacs, who lived next door to us in Ely, begged my mother to bring her to the ranch whenever Mom went to town for supplies. She was younger than I was, so I probably thought she was a pest. I asked Mom why she brought Betty to the ranch all the time. "She is no trouble, and she likes to be here," was my mother's answer. My mother knew what I was too young to understand. When Betty's little brother was killed on the sleigh hill the same year we moved to Ely, her mother never was the same. Betty really needed us. She later told me, we helped her through a very bad time in her life.

Three friends regularly came to stay with me on the ranch during my grade school and high school years. Ann Gaufin, Barbara Kaiser, and Karen Grant. Each of them have stories to tell about their stays. Karen and I took the motor scooter to Hot Creek, swimming one afternoon with the idea that we would get a beautiful tan for a dance we were going to. We made the mistake of taking Bonnie along. (Maybe Mom made us take her.) I hit a rock and wrecked the scooter about halfway there. We were not hurt much, but Bonnie, age eight, refused to get back on the scooter. It was six miles to get home or six miles to go on to Hot Creek. We begged and yelled, but Bonnie refused to go with us. We'd threaten to leave her and start off, but she just sat down in the middle of the gravel road. Finally, we threw her on the scooter, and Karen held her down while she screamed all the way to the swimming pond. After a couple of hours, we had a nice reddish tan color going for us. The night of the dance, however, we called each other in tears. Skin started peeling off our shoulders, arms, and faces in wide strips when we took our showers. We were a mess.

Ann remembers us starting off on our horses for Hiko to see Kathryn Rose. Hiko was seventy-five miles away. Fortunately Ed Rowlie came along in the truck and persuaded us to turn around.

Barbara begged me to cut her hair, so I used the horse clippers. She wore a scarf for weeks. One night as we were tucked into our bedrolls ever the creek, Barb said to me, "Sally, I don't remember any of your cats being black and white." I looked on the creek bank by the foot of our beds about six feet from us to see a skunk. I scooted out of bed very quietly, got the truck, a garden hose, and a bucket of water. That summer those skunks (or civet cats) were everywhere.

My friends didn't mind helping me with the work every day. They have great memories of spending time with me at the ranch. As I got older, I was no longer bored. There was always work to do, and I had no trouble finding things to do whenever I had a free hour or so.

Swimming at Hot Creek

37 My Rich Aunt Mabel

Mabel, my mother's older sister, was the most exciting person in my life. She was very tall and beautiful and rich! She held her long blonde hair in a bun with tortoise shell and sterling silver combs. She wrote me letters from Park Avenue in New York City and sent me postcards from all the places in the world she visited. Mabel came to the ranch a few times where she fussed over me, combing my hair into a bun and dressing me in pretty dresses she had brought me. She had no children, so I was the daughter she never had. She encouraged me to write and saved every letter I ever wrote to her.

Later she visited us in Ely. I carried a picture in my wallet of her standing in a snowdrift in New York City in a mink coat and hat, and all my friends knew about my "Rich Aunt Mabel." When she was the editor of a magazine in NYC, she used Sally Whipple as her pen name for a column she wrote. I got to stay with her for a week. She took me to art and history museums. Quite an experience for a young girl from Sunnyside.

When she could no longer live by herself, I brought her to Carson City where she lived happily in a retirement center for nine years. I loved caring for her until she died at age ninety-six. After her death in 2005, old photos and stacks of notes and letters in a box under her marble coffee table, bought in the 1950s in New York City, gave me the clues to the story of her life. She had written who was in each picture, and where and when it was taken, on the back of every photo. It was easy to piece together her life by going through her notes and photos and finding a time line she had made of her life. I had been intrigued with Aunt Mabel's stories my whole life. After finding a poem she'd written in 1979, I decided I needed to write her story.

Rummaging in the attic
Of my yester years
And shedding
Up to date tears.

Mabel graduated from White Pine High School in 1927. Before she graduated, she signed a contract to teach in Cobre, Nevada. That was illegal because she was not yet eighteen and had not had any college classes, but the father of two boys she knew in high school was on the Cobre School Board, and they could not find anybody else who would agree to teach in Cobre. She did go to summer school in Logan, Utah, that summer. This was called Normal School, and after completing twelve weeks of classes, she was certified to teach.

In the fall of 1927, on her eighteenth birthday, Mabel boarded the Nevada Northern Railway in Ely and headed north ninety miles to Cobre where the Northern Nevada met with the Southern Pacific on its cross-country freight and passenger trip. The train crossed miles and miles of sagebrush and greasewood before it arrived in Cobre. The welcoming committee was impressive. Students, ages six to sixteen were lined up in clean, but faded overhauls along the depot wall. There were two white kids. The rest were Mexican, Japanese, and Italian. Each of their faces were scrubbed to a fine shine. A stern tall man escorted her to the station, placed her two bags on a cart to be pushed down the track to her new home. She lived on the top floor of an imposing two-story wooden building with a HOTEL AND EATS sign tacked on the side, slightly askew. Inside was a bar, a grill, and a pool table. Either the builder didn't know how to build inside staircases or forgot to build one. She, at risk of losing her life, had to crawl up the outside of the building to the second floor, always fearful the tacked-on stairs would separate from the wall. Fifteen or more trains clanged, hissed, and whistled their way through the middle of town all day and night. As she settled into her small room, she realized she was about to begin her life as a responsible adult.

She taught sixteen students, all eight grades. At night she taught some of the adults. During that school year, she birthed a Mexican baby when the father appeared at her door asking for her help. In his mind, a teacher should be able to do anything. She found a dead man in the brush as she was hiking around after the spring thaw. An eight-year-old Mexican boy was shot by a Mexican worker. A passenger from the Southern Pacific died from epilepsy at the Cobre Depot, and the telegraph dispatcher tried to attack her by chasing her around a table when she was cutting out a dress. On payday, most of the men spent their two-week paychecks at the hotel drinking and gambling. She lived there four months before she comprehended the meaning of the word Cobre—"stung many times." She taught only one year at Cobre and then came home to her parent's ranch at Baker for the summer. She then went to the University of Nevada in Reno from September 1928–June 1929.

Again she came back to Baker for the summer. That summer she got engaged to Byron Tilby, a boy from Jerome, Idaho, who had come to Baker to stay with his aunt and uncle. Fall came and Byron returned to Idaho while Mabel stayed home and taught grades one through five at Baker, five miles from the ranch where her parents and sisters lived. She spent the following summer in Idaho with Byron but returned to teach another year at Baker believing that Byron would come back to his aunt and uncle's the following summer and he and Mabel would be married. He did not come back, so she mailed his ring back to him immediately. A few years ago she told me Byron Tilby was the love of her life. That summer of 1930, she began dating my father and apparently accepted a ring from him, but Daddy found out she was seeing someone else (probably Byron), and they broke up.

On August 30, her "twenty-first" birthday, she met a young man named Ed Rott. A friend had brought him to her birthday party which was held at Lehman Caves a few miles from her home. Everyone needed to climb into it on ladders at that time. He offered to drive her to Current Creek the following day, because she had signed a contract to teach there for the 1930-1931 school year. They began dating and were married in December.

When school was out, they moved to Berkeley, California, where they lived with Ed's parents for almost four years. He sold car insurance and Mabel sold encyclopedias in San Francisco. Neither of them were happy, so when Ed got a federal grant to map Indian reservations in the Southwest United States, they were very ready to start a new chapter in their lives.

For three years they lived in a tent and moved around from the Hopi, Walpi, Apache, and Navajo Indian Reservations. Throughout those years, Mabel spent her days doing woodworking, reading and exploring the mesas, collecting fascinating pieces of broken Indian pottery. Few white people lived on the reservations, so my six-foot tall aunt was an especially curious creature in her pants and knee-high boots as she hiked around the mesas.

The fourth year they were there they bought a small silver house trailer. Out there that was the equivalent of moving from a one room apartment to a mansion. The bedroom had two cots and a shelf for the gasoline lantern.

The other room had a gasoline two-burner stove and a card table with two chairs. They used wooden crates to store their canned goods. Every two weeks, they'd head to Gallop, New Mexico, in their trusty pickup to get supplies. They kept cool in the 110-degree weather by putting a big chunk of dry ice, bought at the filling station, on the floor of the truck. The heat was unbearable. In Chandler, they made a swamp cooler for the bedroom window by dripping water over straw between wire which kept the entire house cool. As an afterthought, they attacked a shower overhead. Cockroaches two inches long raced over their feet. Mabel managed to lock herself in the outhouse one day and after screaming for some time, Ed came and removed the latch to get her out.

At 2:30 one afternoon, Mabel answered a knock on the side door of the trailer in a lavender nightgown. Joseph Shaffhausen stood at the door. The fact that she remembered the time and what she was wearing tells me there was probably an immediate attraction between the two of them. He and his wife, Florence, lived in Chandler in a nearby adobe house.

Between 1934 and 1937, Ed and Mabel had gone to Gallup and Albuquerque, New Mexico; Oklahoma, Washington DC, Phoenix; Sells, San Xavier, Tuscan and Kingman, Arizona; Colorado, Idaho, and Wyoming.

Ed got transferred to Denver in 1937. They sold the trailer after Mabel had pulled it by herself from San Xavier to Denver. Mabel then drove alone from Denver to Baker, where she stayed a few weeks before going on to Reno for another semester of college from September to December 1937. The time and place is right to assume that was when Ruth, Mabel's youngest sister, caught Mabel and Byron Tilby together. Ruth was married to Byron, and they had Orvis, who was about sixteen months old. Ruth divorced him that same year, 1937.

At Christmas time Mabel went to Berkeley where she and Ed again lived with his parents until he got a job as a geologist and left for Colombia, South America; in February, Mabel joined him the following July.

She traveled by herself to New York City by train for five days and four nights and stayed with her best friends, Joseph and Florence Shaffhausen in Dobbs Ferry, New York, for a week before she booked passage on the Grace Line Motor Ship, Santa Maria, from New York through the Panama Canal to Buenaventura, Colombia, on July 29, 1938. From there she went by train over the Andes Mountains to Ibague.

Ed spent much of his time in the jungle, but Mabel had many friends and a full life for the fifteen months she lived there. She lived in a two-story villa, in Ibague, and she had a maid. She was given a white puppy as a gift, had a larger dog, a monkey and an ocelot, a pet tiger, named Tigra, to keep her company. When she bought her horse, Siva, she didn't realize it was a jumper. She then learned to jump him. Mabel spent time with the American friends from the colony in Ibague. They once rode a cable car down the Magdalena River, and they rode horses and had picnics in the Andes. She even learned a little bit about archery.

Then Ed made a trip back to the United States in September 1939 which changed Mabel's whole life. When he returned to Ibague, he told Mabel he'd gotten a vasectomy. He had not consulted with her or even told her he'd planned to do it. She sold her horse, got rid of her pets, left Ed, and came back to the United States on a ship up the west coast.

Her life was in shambles. She arrived in San Francisco with $1000, knowing nobody and with no job. As she was walking around looking for a job, she found a rental bookstore for sale. The cost of $900 included two small rooms in the back where she could live. She bought it. It was a cold and dark place, and few people came to rent books. She knew nothing about running a business or renting books. She only knew she'd read most of the books in the bookstore. When the old lady who sold the place to Mabel came back from a cruise and agreed to buy the store back, Mabel called the University of Nevada to see if there was a school in Nevada that needed a teacher for the spring semester, 1940. Yes, Mountain City needed a teacher. She took her possessions to Baker and left for Elko on New Year's Day where she was met by the father of three of the four kids she would teach and was driven to Mountain City. She was to stay with the man and his family, but when she climbed the stairs with a kerosene lamp to her bedroom and sat on the bed, it broke. She yelled down that she was leaving, but the man rushed to fix the bed. The next day she threatened to leave again when she learned she was to walk a mile in the snow to the schoolhouse which hadn't been used in five years and was filthy. A trailer was immediately brought in, so she stuck it out until summer.

In the fall she was offered a teaching job at Kimberly outside of Ely. Over Easter break, friends drove her to Elko to get a divorce from Ed. She did not sign a teaching contract for the next year, but instead, left for New York when her friends, Joseph and Florence, suggested she needed to start a new life. She stayed in New York City for twenty-seven years.

In the 1940s, Mabel worked for an advertising agency, The March of Dimes, and an agriculture association where she was the editor and publisher of the *Farm Builder Magazine*. She eventually became president of the company. Nobody knew she was a woman until the first board meeting because she signed her name M. F. Robison.

Soon after she got to New York City, Mabel and Joseph began a seventeen-year affair. She remained friends with Florence and thought of Joseph's kids as her own. In 1954, Florence, Mabel, and Caroline, Joseph's daughter, took a trip to Italy and Spain.

Mabel was able to get an apartment on Park Avenue when Maude, an old lady who lived in the flat next to her, died and left Mabel a fortune in stocks. Mabel had been bringing her food and caring for her because she believed she was destitute. The Park Avenue apartment had servants' quarters and gilded faucets and fixtures.

In the 1950s, Joseph (who was president of the Martin Steel Company) and Mabel flew all over the United States in the company plane, an aero commander 500. Joseph was always going to divorce Florence, but it never happened. When Florence got cancer in 1955, Mabel gave up and began dating other men even though she still continued to see Joseph.

Finally in 1960, she married Dolf Fritsche. Joseph fell apart and immediately filed for divorce. Mabel left Dolf, came to Nevada, and got a divorce in Las Vegas then returned to New York City to wait for Joseph's New York divorce (which would take a year) to be final. In October, four months before the divorce was final, he dropped dead of a heart attack while attending a business conference in Bridgeport, Connecticut. Mabel was sitting beside him.

At that time Mabel was the vice president of the Martin Steel Company, vice president and secretary of Agricultural Associates as well as one of three directors, a director and secretary of Schaffhausen Corporation, and a director and secretary of Martin Sales Company. She was in *Who's Who among American Women*. She resigned from all her business connections, gave up her apartment in November, and took a freighter to the Virgin Islands by herself until January when she came back and remarried Dolf. I once asked Dolf why he agreed to remarry Mabel, and he said in his heavy German accent, "I shust luvt dat big grl."

Mabel and Dolf moved to Phoenix in 1963 when my father asked them to manage his apartment complex. They stayed in Phoenix until Dolf died. Warner, Bonnie, and I then packed Mabel's things and brought her to Carson City in 1996. She later wrote, *I am happy Sally and Warner packed me up and moved me here. I had a reservation about living in this "holding pen for the aged" but now I like it here. Nice apartment really. I'm glad I'm out of Phoenix.*

Mabel died on March 15, 2005. She was content to live in a studio apartment with her many treasures she had collected throughout her lifetime. She had gold boxes and rose and green jade statues, a handwoven afghan from India, cloisonne lamps, Chinese pottery lamps, expensive original paintings, and her precious elephant collection from everywhere in the world.

Her memory got bad, but she was otherwise very healthy until her last five weeks when she got congestive heart failure, and I had to put her in a nursing home. She handled all the problems of old age with the same positive attitude, grace, and courage that I admired and loved about her all of my life. I found a scrap of paper in one of her boxes on which she had written *"I hope Sally will be the one to care for me when I get aged and 'dotty'..."* I am happy I was the one.

Mabel visiting at the ranch

Mabel wearing mink coat in New York City

Mabel in Colombia, South America

38   *The Fun of Dying*

"He beat us," Bonnie says as we drive over the knoll above the Lund cemetery. We see Warner's truck parked down by the fence, and we see our brother talking to someone over by our family plot. "There seems to be quite a few people and not too much wind," I say. "This is going to be a fun year."

Some of the coldest days of my life have been spent at this cemetery. The wind gets started up north in the mountains around Ely which is almost seven thousand feet above sea level. There is nothing to stop the gales as they blow through the White River Valley which must be over two hundred miles long. Except for the wind and the cold, any native Nevadan should love to be buried at the Lund cemetery. There is a fenced off pasture with Nevada desert as far as you can see surrounding it on two sides, farmland and the small community of Lund on the other two sides, and mountains to the far east and to the west. Lilacs and yellow roses have been planted along the fence line. On a few lucky Memorial Days the lilacs and roses have been blooming.

Each year I fly to Las Vegas where my sister, Bonnie, and I prepare a picnic and drive the three hours north to Lund. Warner meets us from Elko and brings the drinks (except when he forgets). In the old days, all our family would meet at our Uncle Vern's beautiful old home for a picnic. He and Aunt Luella are now in the cemetery with plastic flowers arranged carefully over them.

We drive down and park next to several other cars, stretch our legs, and enter the cemetery. The first thing I do is look for any fresh mounds of dirt. My cousin Dean has pointed out to me where his plot is. He is proud to have it because it is in the shade of the only tree in the cemetery.

"If you show up some year, Sal," he told me, "and you see fresh dirt

215

over there, don't look for me up top; just throw a few of your flowers over that way."

I walk to my brother, and we greet with a handshake (which is equivalent to a hug in our family). He asks what took us so long, and we begin the yearly cemetery ritual. We start at the family plot where Grandpa and Grandma are side by side to the east of Mom and Dad. Two more plots within this family lot that my grandfather purchased years ago are empty. I have made sure that one has been saved for me, and I think Warner will be in the other one although he won't say for sure. He keeps saying that I have "yammered" at him all of his life, and he doesn't want to get close enough for me to continue the yammering after we die. It is his way, I think, of telling me he loves me.

This year we notice that Dad's grave has begun to sink, and we had to find our cousin JL, who is the grave keeper, to tell him he needs to lift up the sod and put a little dirt underneath.

"I'll do it myself if you've got a shovel around," Warner tells him.

As I look at these graves, I remember an incident which we laugh about now but which wasn't as funny at the time. A relative had stopped us at the top of the hill coming down to the cemetery after our mother's funeral.

"JL did not dig the grave big enough," he told us. "We can't get the casket in the ground yet." We looked down to see a backhoe crawling slowly across the field toward the cemetery. JL was driving it in his black suit. As a member of the priesthood, he had dedicated the grave a short time earlier according to Mormon tradition. Then we had all driven back up to the church in Lund where a huge feast had been prepared for all those who had attended my mother's funeral. Finally our family was going back down to see the grave before we started back to Las Vegas to attend to the sad job of sorting Mom's things. We waited and watched as JL used the backhoe to enlarge the hole, and then several men placed the coffin into the hole. Someone waved to us, and we continued to the cemetery while JL drove the backhoe back to Lund.

We now continue strolling through the pasture, commenting on graves and greeting others who have come with flowers. Most of the decorations are plastic or silk and need to be solidly staked down or the wind will take them to the next valley. Then I see Dean.

"I see you're still up here," I say to him.

He reckons he has made it through another year, and he tells me that I seem to have "wintered" well too. This is a term our grandfather used to describe his cattle.

"Everyone is in just about the same place as they were last year," I observe.

"Yup," Dean says. "Even the ones on top."

Dean's wife, Dixie, and my cousin Lois will come back to the cemetery in two or three days and pick up all the flowers from the graves of our family and store them in their houses until next year. They bring them all back each year, and we may or may not add new arrangements to what was there before. Several aunts and uncles are buried here as well as our parents and grandparents, and we always make sure their graves are decorated nicely.

For the first time, I notice a gravestone with "Mrs. L. Hendrix" and her dates. I realize this is my father's oldest sister's grave who died at age thirty, leaving two young children. I have recently written a book on each of my aunts and uncles and grandparents, and I recognize the dates on the stone. I am sad to see that nobody thought it necessary to put her given name, Eliza Dent, on that stone. We have never even noticed or decorated her grave before. We'll make sure there are flowers on her grave from now on.

It is getting lunchtime and time for our picnic. This is one of the years that Warner forgets to bring the drinks, so we drive to the only store in Lund and buy us each a soda, and Warner decides we should picnic above Lund out of the wind. When we get our blanket down and our picnic spread out, we become aware that this is the Lund dump. My friends at work think I am strange enough to take a day off work to come so far for a picnic in a cemetery. What will they think when I tell them we had picnic at the Lund dump this year?

We begin to talk about the many experiences we've had on Memorial Days and at the funerals which preceded the burial of each one of the relatives at the Lund Cemetery. My earliest memory was coming to my Aunt Beulah's house in Lund early on a Memorial Day so I could help my aunt and cousins make crepe paper flowers to take to the graves. Every inch inside my aunt's house was covered with strips of crepe paper, shavings of paper, and pieces of wire. My aunt had been making flowers for weeks. I didn't get very good at making the flowers, but there were so many that the few faulty ones I contributed were never noticed. We boxed them up and drove down to the cemetery. It began to rain—sideways from the north. The sky was dark, and the wind howled. We were all standing with our backs to the wind, and there was nothing we could do with all those crepe paper flowers except watch the rain wash the color from the crepe paper onto the graves. Years later I had a dream that Warner had died, and the crepe paper flowers were running onto his grave just like that day in Lund.

Mormon funerals always mean food: the pineapple, cottage cheese lime Jello salad, potato and cheese casserole (funeral potatoes), homemade rolls, baked ham, applesauce cake, and at least eight varieties of cookies. In fact, in Lund there is a committee of women who at a moment's notice are able to prepare food for a hundred people whenever there is a funeral. The food is served in the church multipurpose room where tables and chairs are set up. We eat and we tell stories. We talk about the death and the funeral, and we talk about other funerals and then we tell more stories. "I'll never forget the time . . ." or "Remember when . . ." we say as we sit around and visit with our cousins.

One year we had a Whipple family reunion at Preston, near Lund, and we enlisted the same funeral food committee to prepare one of our meals. Someone commented that they hadn't had food this good since Uncle Al died.

"Yup," JL agreed, "seems a darn shame that we have all this good food and nobody has even died."

Mom was the only one who was late for her own funeral. I play an important role in these funerals because I am the one who plans them. There is stress involved to make sure that everything comes off smoothly. Mormon funerals are all done by lay people and usually they are done beautifully. Everything was covered for Mother's funeral—programs made up, speakers chosen, songs and singers selected, special prayers arranged for.

The morning of the funeral, we drove the thirty miles from Ely to the church in Lund, but the hearse was not there yet. I frantically called the mortuary in Ely and was informed that the hearse had left Ely an hour ago. We had traveled the same road and had not run across a broken down hearse (not something you wouldn't notice). What could have happened? Others in my family found this funny, but I was frantic. It was time for her funeral, and my mother had not arrived. Finally, we could see the hearse making its way slowly down the only street in Lund. The mortician backed up to the back door of the church, the casket was unloaded, and the service began. I never asked why they were late.

Even though it was rainy and cold, Dad was on time for his funeral, but it was one of the few Mormon funerals I have attended that did not meet my expectations. First of all, rain was pouring down in sheets. My cousin Keith was driving up the Sunnyside shortcut from Hiko, and he was late. When he arrived he called me aside to tell me that he could not give the eulogy as planned because my father had spoken to him in a dream the night before, and he wanted to relate this experience to the congregation. I quickly found someone else to do the eulogy, but without much preparation it was not the best. Then the bishop of the church in Lund gave a speech. I cannot ever remember asking him to do so, but he began to carry on about his love for one of my dad's sisters, Caroline. He told of seeing her for the first time and how it was love at first sight. We kept waiting for him to mention our father, but he apparently did not even know our father, and he sat down without doing much more than stating Dad's name. It turned out okay because beautiful western and spiritual songs were sung by the ladies in the Mormon church, and of course, the food served afterward was superb.

Then a miracle happened that day. Just as we were getting out of our cars to walk to Daddy's grave, the sky cleared and the sun shone down and warmed all of us clear into our hearts. My daughter, Lesley, age thirteen, observed this closely and then whispered to me, "God is sure smiling; Grandpa must have just made it to heaven."

One year we had a family reunion at Hiko, and our Aunt LaRue was dying just fifty miles away at Caliente. There was talk that we should go ahead with the service because we were all together and would all just have to come back again when she actually died. Our family is just bizarre enough to have gone through with this plan when Aunt LaRue died.

We are needing to get ready to leave, so we begin cleaning up the picnic. It is easy to dispose of our garbage since we are in the Lund dump already. Bonnie and I shake Warner's hand, and we head home. We always enjoy the annual day we spend with our relatives both under and above the ground at the Lund Cemetery. Today was no exception.

Memorial Day - Lund Cemetary

39   *My Hands or a Nice Pair of White Cotton Gloves*

When I lived on the ranch, my hands were an inconvenience to me. When we moved to Ely they became an embarrassment. Finally, in high school and college, they became a disability. The problem was that my hands were icy cold, and they dripped sweat. I mean when I held my hands down, sweat would drip off the end of each finger. I wasn't able to write, read, sew, or play the piano because the paper and fabric and piano keys would become so saturated that I couldn't work anymore. One summer a hired man brought his wife to live on the ranch, and she taught me to crochet. I loved crocheting, but I had to sit on the bridge over the creek, keep the ball of thread in my lap, and crochet over the cold water so my hands wouldn't sweat.

By the time I started high school, my hands were well known among my classmates. I went to only one dance in high school. When I was a freshman, the boy who asked me to dance took my hand and walked me to the dance floor. "My gosh, your hands are cold," he said. He let go of my hand because not only was it cold, it was dripping wet. As we began to dance, the wet spot on his shirt sleeve where my hand rested grew larger and larger until his entire right sleeve was stuck to his arm. He said nothing to me, just walked me back to the bleachers and turned away, wiping at his arm. I called my dad to come take me home.

"Just get yourself a nice pair of white cotton gloves, Sis," my dad said to me when I told him I would never go to another dance again as long as I lived. How could dads be so out of touch? I could never show up at a high school dance wearing a pair of white cotton gloves. Never! From then on, I would only stand at the door of the gymnasium keeping my coat or jacket on just in case anyone who had not heard about my hands asked me to dance. "Thanks," I would say, "but my dad is waiting outside for me."

I loved going to the ranch every weekend. There were no situations there where someone might need to touch my hands. It was the only place I could be where I didn't need to be constantly hiding my hands or holding a tissue.

My hand problem got so bad during my first year at Utah State University, I told Warner I could not continue classes, and I certainly could not stay in the sorority my father had insisted I join. I couldn't write or even hold a book to read. The pages were soaked after five minutes. It had become impossible for me to do writing assignments and especially to take tests. I'd buy a desk-sized ink blotter, cut it into three-inch squares and stack the squares on top of each other, but the pieces would be soaked through before I got halfway down the page. It was hard for me to drive my brother's car when he lent it to me because two puddles of water formed on each side of me on the seat from the sweat that ran down my arms and off my elbows.

Warner called my parents, and they drove to Logan and took me to a doctor in Salt Lake City. He told them I could have my sympathetic gland removed which would stop my hands from sweating, but that wouldn't cure my nervous condition, and I might start stuttering or something else; he suggested a psychiatrist. Warner drove me from Logan to Salt Lake City to see a very expensive psychiatrist ($35 for half an hour) every week until school was out.

I continued seeing the psychiatrist through the summer. My dad and I would fly from the ranch to Salt Lake City in our Cessna 172 airplane. The best part of that was I flew the plane and earned hours toward my private pilot certificate. He'd rent a car and drive me to the doctor, wait in the office while I had my session, drive us back to the airport, and we'd fly back to the ranch. It was haying season and leaving for even a day was hard to do. My dad did not believe in psychiatry, but he wanted me to get better, and all his encouraging talks and letters did not seem to be working to help me. My father wrote this letter to me on May 13, 1957. 8:00 p.m.

> *Dear Sally,*
> *I just dropped you a card but I don't have anything else to do so will write you a little note also. We are stopped at Lubbock at the present time. The elevation is 3256 ft. the sign says. I arrive at Dallas at 9:55 my time 10:55 Dallas time. This country down here is all flat. You can see for a long ways. I hope they don't have any more of those rain storms while I am here. The stewardess lives in Dallas and she didn't know if she would have a home left or not. Evidently she wasn't home last night.*

Sally, you had better quit your worrying about things. You sure don't have anything to worry about. If you would quit worrying your hands wouldn't bother you nearly as much. You just upset yourself to much over your hands, and the more you do the worse they get. Just don't let them bother you so much. Go out and have a good time. When you do go out wear gloves and don't pay attention to them. You certainly have everything to be proud of yourself. Everybody likes you and thinks you are just about it. So you better start thinking the same. Don't get an infferiority (can't spell it) complex just because of your hands. I know it is not pleasant but the more you stew about them the worse they get. I am sure proud of you and I want you to get out and enjoy yourself and have fun. Good clean fun. So just spunk up and say to heck with that. Don't let it get you down. I know everything will turn out all right.

Love, Dad

I can't remember much about those therapy sessions. The doctor didn't think I was able to talk to my parents about my problems, but I thought I wouldn't have any problems if I could just stay on the ranch. He wrote page after page as I talked, but I don't know what I talked about. Finally, one session he stopped writing, looked up and said, "You know, you are very bright."

That comment changed everything for me. I had believed that if I needed to see a psychiatrist, I had mental problems, and mental problems meant I was stupid. So now I concluded that if I was smart, I didn't need this doctor to solve my problems. I walked out of the doctor's office that day and announced to my father that I would not be coming back. A huge smile came over his face. "I know you are going to be just fine, Sis." We drove to the airport for the last time. I don't know if the psychiatrist helped me, but I did begin to believe that nothing going on in my life should ever cause me to get so nervous and upset.

As much as I hated my hand problem, I realize it was not as bad as many problems other people had to deal with. I wish I'd had the maturity in my young life to have taken my father's advice and just worn "a nice pair of white cotton gloves." If my hands were sweaty today, I would wear gloves whenever I needed to, in every color, and not think a thing of it.

40 *A College Education*

My dad wanted me to go to college. "If you're going to marry an educated man, you need to go to college," he told me. I, personally, had no thought that I needed an education or a marriage, but due to some major flaw in my personality, I always did what my dad thought I should do.

The logical choice for a school was Utah State University at Logan, Utah, because that was where Warner was going, and several of the kids from Ely chose to go to Utah State too. I loaded my hoopskirts and my yards and yards of dirndl petticoats into the trunk of Warner's car; and Orvis (our cousin), Warner, and I headed for Logan in the fall of 1956 where I would be staying in a residence hall apartment with five other girls. Shari, my future sister-in-law, was one of the girls. She had announced in her senior year at White Pine High School that she was going to go to Utah State, live with Sally, and marry Warner.

Each apartment had three bedrooms, two girls per bedroom, a large kitchen, and a bathroom. We rotated weekly chores between cooking dinner, cleaning the kitchen after dinner, and cleaning the bathroom. There was a large sitting room where girls from the entire hall entertained their boyfriends or other visitors. We were the first students to live at Moen Hall, so the place was clean and beautiful. The rent was $70 per quarter. Warner, Orvis, and some of our Ely buddies lived in a motel up the street. I had no experience living around people, so I was terribly unhappy. I spent quite a bit of time trying to find a place where I could be alone.

Being the dedicated student that I was, I immediately enrolled in tennis, social dance, basic cloth construction (sewing), photography, skiing, and private pilot certification. Every morning before anyone else in our apartment woke up, I trekked up to the airfield above the campus for my flying lesson. Most mornings, it was dark. There was deep snow to walk through and a biting wind in my face. Still, I never missed a lesson; it was my favorite class. I took lessons all the four quarters that I went to Utah State.

I was informed that English 101 was required, so I reluctantly added it to my curriculum along with a journalism class. It turned out that, surprisingly, the English class was my favorite class because I had a wonderful teacher, Moyle Q. Rice.

Our first assignment, due in two weeks, was our autobiography. I rushed to my room and typed out my life story on my new Smith Corona typewriter. The following week, Mr. Rice announced he would read one story in its entirety written by a student. "This young lady has never been anywhere or done anything in her life, yet she wrote a fascinating story. I got so caught up in the story that I forgot to proofread it," he said. My face turned red, and my hands began to drip sweat as he started reading my story. After that I could do no wrong in his class even though my papers came back dripping with red ink. He always wrote a paragraph in black ink at the end of each of my pieces—phrasing its content. I had never taken a class in all my years in school that I liked. Nor had I ever had a teacher who encouraged me about anything I did until I met Mr. Rice. For the first time in my life, I'd found something I might be good at in the way of education. I was now sure I would be heading abroad as a famous journalist.

For extracurricular activities, Shari and I went to Alta and Brighton skiing with Warner, Orvis, and their buddies several times. I never learned to ski very well, but I loved being with the guys from Ely and riding the lift to the top of the mountain. Everyone else had brand-new Head skis and top equipment, but everything I was using was hand-me-downs. I remember ducking from the Ski Patrol because I didn't have safely bindings, and that was illegal. The joke was Warner would stop by the infirmary at the end of the day to pick me up because I got carried off the mountain so many times.

Quite often, Warner would drive us all to Salt Lake City to movies. We all sat in a long row to see *Oklahoma* one Saturday afternoon. Warner and I had never heard of a musical, so we thought we were seeing a good old western movie when we looked at the marquee. About halfway through the movie, Warner announced loudly enough for most of the people in the theater to hear, "If that son of a bitch gets up on that haystack and starts singing, I'm out'a here." Sure enough Gordon MacRae (Curly) jumped on the haystack and began singing "Oh, What a Beautiful Mornin." Warner stood up and marched out of the theater. He had the car, so the whole row of us stood up and filed out behind him. I've never seen the rest of *Oklahoma* to this day.

Even though I missed the ranch terribly, I think I could have gotten through my first year of college without a nervous breakdown if my dad hadn't decided I needed to join a sorority. I needed to learn to be around people and socialize more, he told me. Everything about that experience from the "exchanges" where we were told to mix with the fraternity boys at socials to formal dances where we had to invite a boy was traumatic for me. I once agreed to learn the hula for a Hawaiian social at the sorority house, but I left the lesson in tears because my hands were sweating so bad I couldn't hold the two rocks we were clicking together. I then refused to take part in many of the activities and had to wax the chapter room floor for my insubordination. One memorable senior sorority sister named Lesley Hall was especially kind to me. I never forgot her and named my daughter Lesley Kathryn after her.

I can't tell the whole story of my year at Utah State without telling about *the Duck Hunt*. Glenna, from Moroni, Utah, (the only person more naive than Glenna from Moroni, Utah, was Sally from Sunnyside, Nevada) hated sorority life as much as I did. One night we sneaked to the basement of the sorority house, climbed out a window, and started to walk back to Moen Hall. Two fellows stopped to see if we wanted a ride back to the dorm, and since it was very cold, we accepted. One of the guys had a great idea. "Do you gals want to go down in the field below Logan duck hunting with us?" What I remember is that duck hunting was the first thing I'd been invited to do that I knew I'd enjoy. We accepted their invitation without reservation. They went back to their apartment and while we waited in the car, they got their shot guns and waders. Glenna then ended up in the front seat with the driver, and I sat in the backseat with the other guy as we headed to the lower fields below Logan. When we stopped at a gate, Glenna and I sat waiting for someone to get out and open the gate. That did not happen. Both boys simultaneously attacked us. They were on top of us pulling at our clothes, and we were screaming. I was also biting, kicking, and pulling hair. Suddenly the one attacking me sat up and angrily told the driver to take these stupid little @#$%@ back to the campus. They could have left us in the field, so we were grateful that they waited until we were through the campus gate before they kicked us out the car doors. We ran home, both of us hysterical. My roommates (including Shari) made me a hot bath and tried to soothe me. I swore everybody to secrecy because I was so embarrassed to have been so stupid, but it did not end there.

The next day the buzzer at my apartment rang, and I found five of my buddies from Ely at the door. "Hi, Sally," Orvis said. "We wondered if you'd like to go duck hunting with us." They never let me live that down, and I never really forgave Shari for rushing out to tell them.

My hand problem got so bad I couldn't write or even hold a book to read. The pages were soaked after five minutes. Taking a test was impossible. Even my English class with Moyle Q. Rice and my morning hike to the airport for flying lessons didn't keep me from wanting to go home. Truthfully, I was embarrassed that Warner had to drive me to Salt Lake City every week to a psychiatrist. I couldn't see any improvement in my hands either.

Looking back, I remember several girls who had almost as hard a time adjusting to dorm life as I did. We should have all carpooled to the psychiatrist, I think. Marva Ann, a junior, was bulimic. We laughed at her when she'd go into the bathroom and stick her finger down her throat because nobody had heard of bulimia then. Priscilla waited for her missionary boyfriend to return and then was jilted. She cried for months. Shari had eczema so bad I had to rub a sheep-dip smelling tar into her hair every night and then try to wash it out every morning before she went to class. One girl upstairs refused to get out of bed for weeks until her parents finally came and took her home.

I didn't go back to Utah State the next year mostly because of the sorority. Warner and I both stayed on the ranch and didn't go to college at all the fall semester of 1957. My hands got better. Then one day Daddy showed up at the ranch and announced, "Sally, you need to go to college somewhere and find a man." Since I had just learned that Johnny Adams was getting married, and since I did everything my dad asked, I did continue my education, and I did, eventually, find an educated man.

Sally (in front right with blonde hair) at Moen Hall/Utah State University

Warner, Sally and Orvis heading to Utah State

41 Dying—One Cousin at a Time

Dean would get a kick out of the fact that he'd died on the knoll above the Lund Cemetery. He'd probably tell us to just roll him down the hill into his plot. We were all shocked to hear of his death because his lean tall structure, salt and pepper hair, and beautiful smile made him one of the healthiest looking and most handsome of my boy cousins. It's funny that I think of them as my boy cousins when most of them are in their seventies, and two are over eighty years old. Dean was seventy-six.

I last saw him at our 2009 family reunion in Hiko where Dean, my cousin Jack, and I sat visiting under the trees. Jack's mother, my dad's oldest sister, died of blood poisoning leaving Jack, age four, and Zelda, age two to be raised by the Whipple family. Jack told me he had lived with his grandparents and every one of his aunts and uncles, including my mom and dad, sometime in his young life. Murray was his favorite. He taught Jack to rope and ride and was always joking and happy. He was devastated when news reached him in 1945 while he was overseas that Murray had died.

"I know everybody liked Murry," Dean said to us that night. "But I always liked and admired your dad, Uncle Punk. We had to work hard for him, but he treated us well. Sunnyside was the best kept ranch anywhere around. I've tried to model my life after him." He then told of coming home from school to find my dad's truck in front of their house. His dad (Uncle Vern) told him to get his things together because he was going to Sunnyside to help Uncle Punk.

"Did you want to go?" I asked. "Did you get paid?"

"I never even thought about it," Dean answered. "Uncle Punk needed help at Sunnyside, so I just went with him. Besides I loved that ranch."

Later, Dean bought his own place in Lund. The day he died, he was bringing his last load of hay for the day from Cave Valley to Lund. A man driving behind him saw him swerve to the side of the road and slump over the

231

steering wheel. He rushed to him, but although one foot was on the clutch and one was on the brake and the engine was still running, Dean was dead.

We all arrived in Lund for the viewing at 12:00 noon and for the funeral at 1:00. Warner wasn't in any hurry to get there. "How can it take an hour to view him?" He wanted to know. We walked past the casket then went into the chapel and sat down. As more and more people came into the church, men began setting up folding chairs in the back until there was no more floor space. Everybody in Lund came to the funeral as well as most of his family from out of town. He had lived in Lund all of his life, and his family now owned the only store in Lund. He had four kids and seventeen grandkids who all lived in Lund or close by. He and Dixie had been married for fifty-four years.

I saw people I hadn't seen for forty years. I saw an old man with part of his face missing, and I remembered he was the kid who'd bitten a stick of dynamite in Cave Valley fifty years ago. I saw the son of the man who drove the mail truck to Sunnyside each week. He remembered me as a little skinny white-haired girl who was always barefoot. And I saw Shirley Peacock who'd come to the ranch to help my mother after she had fainted one morning from exhaustion. I still remember a bracelet with a beautiful blue stone she gave me.

Two of Dean's daughters and his daughter-in-law spoke first. Every story they told about him revealed the two most important things in his life—his family and his work ethic. Many of the same stories could have been told about my family. The kids were expected to work, but they were treated with love and respect. The girls were expected to be ladies. Unlike my father, Dean believed a girl could be a cowgirl and a lady at the same time, and his daughters were very involved with the horses and cattle.

Next the grandkids told about a memory they had of their grandfather. One granddaughter explained that Dean utilized all his grandchildren on branding day. They were to throw the calves and hold them down while he branded, earmarked, and castrated them. "He lay his pocketknife on the calf while he branded him," she explained. "We were to hold the calf so still that the knife would not fall into the dirt, and we followed his instructions carefully because we knew this was the same knife he'd be cutting the cheese with at lunch time."

Even though most of his family were all active in the church, Dean did not go to church. He believed he did not need to go to church to have a testimony of God. He had read the Bible, and he told his family he loved everything God created.

One daughter once suggested to her father that their family should have Family Home Evening. Monday night is set aside for time when Mormon families get together for prayer, scripture reading, and family time. No church meetings are ever held on Mondays. Dean answered, "Sure, get your sisters and brother and get in the truck. We'll fix fence as a family." She said they later decided that their family had more Family Home Evenings than any family in Lund. Dean's entire family came to the front of the chapel and sang "Red River Valley." They changed some of the words and called the song "White River Valley."

Dean's plot is near the west fence under one of the few trees in the cemetery where it will be shaded from the afternoon sun. Dean had pointed it out to me several years ago, and I will be putting flowers on his grave every year from now on. I'll cry a few tears for him and my other cousins who've died.

There was never a time on the ranch when there weren't cousins working for my dad. They teased me and threw me or one of my dozen or more cats in the ditch. We got into water fights and went swimming at Hot Creek. I think I'm the girl cousin they know best because I grew up at Sunnyside. I have stayed close to my cousins throughout all our lives.

I remember a family reunion when I was introducing the program. I mentioned to Keith that I needed to "freshen up" before I got in front of the people, and I couldn't find a mirror. Keith and Dean decided they could use the cosmetics in my purse and they could "freshen me up." Using the eye shadow for lipstick and the eyeliner for my eyebrows wasn't too bad. It was when they used the lipstick for eye shadow that I took on a rather unusual look. Of course, I kept it all on to prove that old cowboys have many talents.

My cousins believed I was never afraid of anything.

Even though I'm younger than many of my cousins, this funeral made me realize I am entering the winter of my life. Every one of my aunts and uncles are gone. Now, as of February 2012, four more of my cousins have died, including Jack. When one dies, I feel like a small part of me has died with them.

42 *The Missing Piece*

After having a crush on Johnny Adams for over ten years, he and I finally got together in 1957 on the twenty-fourth of July (the day Lund had a parade, rodeo, and dance to celebrate the Mormons settling in Utah). We spent time together during the short time left of that summer. We were so comfortable together it didn't seem like dating to me. I'd been dreaming for so many years about being with Johnny, it felt like I'd already been with him.

Then one perfect evening while we were sitting in his truck, he pulled me close to him and said, "I'll be leaving for BYU soon. When I get settled, I'll be calling for a pretty little blonde-haired girl to join me." That was the happiest moment of my life. We were going to be married. I couldn't think of anything else for the entire fall, but I didn't tell a soul, not even Warner. I just waited for Tuesdays and Fridays when the mail truck came, hoping and praying for a letter from Johnny. I had already decided to stay on the ranch that semester because I'd almost had a nervous breakdown during my first year of college at Utah State. Warner decided not to go back to college either. September, October, and November went by and I heard nothing from Johnny.

Finally it was December and Warner and I went to the Ely house for Christmas. One morning I saw my cousin Kent's truck out front when I came back from downtown. I rushed up the stone steps to the front door. "What are you guys doing here?" I asked Kent and Leo Stewart when I saw them sitting on the couch in the living room. I was excited to see them because I hadn't really seen anyone except Warner and Ed Rowlie all fall.

Just as I sat down Leo answered me, "Well, it's Christmas break, and we're heading down to Adams' Ranch to give Johnny a bad time. We understand he's engaged."

I stopped breathing. I felt like I'd been punched in the chest. The whole living room turned a greenish hue and began to turn. I'm sure I was white as a sheet because I felt like I'd pass out or throw up, so I jumped up and ran for the back door. I think I was trying to get to the fort I'd built on the hill behind our house, but I have no idea if I made it. I blacked out. Nothing like that has ever happened to me again.

I now realize why I reacted to Leo's news like I did. It was at that moment that all my dreams ended. It was no longer possible to fantasize about living on a ranch with Johnny. The life I'd created all these years in my mind was over. Johnny and I would not be together; we would not be running Sunnyside or any other ranch. Whatever happened from then on would make no difference to me.

I've never had a clear vision of my future since that awful December morning in the living room of the Ely house. What could have gone wrong? I relived that night in Johnny's truck over and over. Finally I decided he hadn't meant to marry me at all. He didn't say, "Will you marry me?" What a fool I'd been. I was so in love with him; I had just imagined he'd asked me to marry him. I even began to feel embarrassed that I had been so naive. *Thank God I never told anyone*, I thought. Other times I'd think something must have happened to make him change his mind, but I believed it would always be a puzzle to me.

Johnny got married in the LDS Temple. Someone told me his wife reminded them of me. He got a teaching degree and taught school in Hawthorne. Then he moved his family to Fallon where he bought a farm, taught school, and became a cattle buyer. He called me once when he heard my mother died, and once I called him to find out about his mother whom I was very close to.

I went on with my rather purposeless life going to college in Santa Barbara that spring semester because Kathryn was going to nursing school there. Then I transferred to UNR where I met and married. Stan and I lived in Alaska for three years then moved to Carson City. We had two children but divorced after eleven years of marriage.

During the eight years I was divorced, while I was dating a teacher who had taught with Johnny Adams at Hawthorne, I found a small piece to my puzzle. "I understand we have a mutual friend . . . Sally Whipple," my boyfriend said to Johnny one night when they met at a ball game.

"Yes," Johnny told him, "I really liked Sally a lot, but I never thought I could deal with her dad." That was it? What did he mean? I didn't think Daddy had much contact with Johnny. His comment did not make any sense to me, but again I believed I never would figure it out.

The years passed by fairly quickly. Out of necessity, I went back to college and got a teaching degree and then a master's in education so I could support my children. I taught for thirty years and retired. By then I had remarried and helped raise two stepdaughters. After thirty years of marriage, I got a divorce and set about living in Carson City in the home and property I'd worked so hard to make into my Sunnyside. But after two divorces, I couldn't help wondering why I didn't get to marry the love of my life. It was still a puzzle to me.

Then almost exactly fifty years after Johnny Adams broke my heart, I found the missing piece to my puzzle. I'd gone with a group of people from Hiko and Alamo on a tour to Branson, Missouri, and Palmyra, New York. Keith invited me to go along because I'd gone to church with many of the Alamo people as a teenager. One of those people was Leo Stewart, and I ended up sitting next to him and his wife on the airplane. I finally decided to ask Leo, "Do you ever hear anything from Johnny Adams?"

"Oh yes," he answered, "I see him quite often. His health isn't real good—some sort of heart condition."

"I was just crazy about him," I said.

"Oh, I know that. And he really liked you. He talked about you often."

I then related to Leo what Johnny had said about my dad many years before. He'd said he didn't feel he could deal with my dad.

"It's true. John had no use for your dad," Leo said. "I always liked your dad, but many people did not because of his fiery temper. In fact, Johnny went to Punk and told him he planned to marry you. Your dad fired back in no uncertain terms, "There is no way in hell you're ever going to marry Sally!"

There it was! I'd found the missing piece of my life on an airplane somewhere between Missouri and New York. Johnny had planned to marry me. Before he left for BYU, and after he'd proposed to me, he'd gone to my dad and told him he planned to marry me. My dad's reaction made him realize he didn't want to spend the rest of his life dealing with Punk Whipple. He believed our marriage would not have worked because of my dad. He was ready to get married, so he'd found somebody else and was engaged by Christmas. It is obvious I was not the love of his life.

"Why would my dad do that?" I asked Keith while we were sitting together on that same trip in an airport waiting for a flight. "He ruined my life. When did my dad ever have much contact with Johnny?"

Keith said he witnessed one incident when Johnny and other cowboys from the Pahranagat and White River Valleys were gathering cattle off the range for the winter. Somebody told my dad they'd seen Keith leave one of Daddy's cows while bringing in his own. There were thousands of acres to search for cattle. Keith was my dad's nephew, and he respected Daddy; he would surely never have left anybody's cow—let alone my dad's. But my dad flew into one of his famous rages.

"You get your outfit and get the hell out of here. Get all your #&@ cattle off this range and start heading south." Then he turned to Johnny and said, "John, you come and help me take my cattle north."

Johnny said, "No, I believe I'll be riding south with Keith." He turned and walked away. This really infuriated my dad. He called Johnny some names and stormed off.

"That was only one instance that I know of," Keith said. "There were probably others. Your dad had quite a reputation for flying off the handle. By the way, he did apologize to me later, but Johnny didn't know about that."

In my father's defense, he had no idea how much I loved Johnny. We didn't talk about such things in our family, so I had never told anyone. That part of my life was my secret.

Looking back, I believe if I had married Johnny, we would still be married. Our families had the same ranching backgrounds, our parents were friends, and we were both the same religion. I was very much in love with Johnny, and now I have reason to believe, at that time, Johnny loved me too. Fifty or so years later, I'm happy for the closure, but things work out the way they are supposed to. It is best Johnny remained the love of my dreams, not the love of my life.

There is one final piece to my life's puzzle, though. I've lived through and somewhat gracefully dealt with all my life's experiences, and I now understand that happiness is not a place or a person. It is a time. The last piece of my life's puzzle is a time . . . a time to reflect and appreciate where I have come from . . . a time to be grateful for the life I've lived . . . a time to enjoy the life I have right now.

CPSIA information can be obtained at www.ICGtesting.com
Printed in the USA
LVOW08s1934120214

373409LV00001B/295/P